Introduction

Exploring the forest is a visual activity, a game or sport that trains the eye. Most budding naturalists soon acquire a copy of one or more of the Field Guides, such as *A Field Guide to the Birds* or *A Field Guide to Wildflowers.* These handy, pocket-sized books offer shortcuts to identification, reducing things to basic shapes and patterns, with arrows pointing to the special "field marks" by which one species can be separated from another.

Although even a person who is colorblind can become skilled at identifying birds by their patterns, and flowers and trees by their leaf-shapes and other structures, for most of us color is the first clue. This coloring book will sharpen your observations and condition your memory for the days you spend in the forest. By filling in the colors during evenings at home or on winter days before the migrants arrive (if you live in the North), or before the flowers and butterflies add color to the landscape, you will be better informed about these same animals and plants when you see them in life. Binoculars are a big help if you have a pair; a seven or eight-power glass makes a bird or mammal seven or eight times as handsome, but is not necessary for plants, insects, or reptiles.

A coloring book such as this will help your color perception, but it will not teach you to draw, unless you copy the basic line drawings so artfully prepared by Sara Bennett. You might even try to sketch things in the field, if only roughly in pencil.

Exploring the forest, watching the birds and other animals, and seeking out the plants, can be many things — an art, a science, a game, or a sport — but above all it is an absorbing activity that sharpens the senses, especially the eye and the ear. If you draw or paint, the sense of touch also comes into play; the images of the eye and the mind are transferred by hand to paper. In the process, you become more aware of the natural world — the real world — and inevitably you become an environmentalist.

Most of you may find colored pencils best suited for coloring this book, but if you are handy with brushes and paints, you may prefer to fill in the outlines with watercolors. Crayons, too, can be used. But don't labor; have fun. That is what woodland exploration and this coloring book are all about.

Roger Tory Peterson

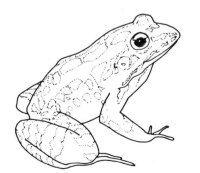

About This Book

The United States is a vast country enriched with an impressive diversity of wildlife. Over 600 species of birds nest within the continental U.S. In many ways the U.S. is a land of forests. As you travel from north to south, coast to coast, or across the various mountain ranges, you are rarely away from trees. Each type of forest has a special look and feeling, the result of the plants and animals that live there. This book is designed to acquaint you with the most important species of plants and animals seen in the many different kinds of forests found throughout the country.

This is not just a book for you to read. It is a *coloring* book and that is how you are meant to use it. By looking at the colored pictures on the front and back covers and reading the descriptions that accompany each picture, you can accurately color every plant and animal in this book. By doing so you will learn much about how to look at nature.

Sir Arthur Conan Doyle's great fictional detective, Sherlock Holmes, was known for his keen ability to note details. What color were a man's shoes? Did he smoke a cigar or pipe? Was he wearing a hat? Holmes was able to solve the most mysterious crimes because he understood the importance of seeing detail rather than simply getting a general impression. Holmes's eye for detail should be developed by everyone who enjoys nature. To be able to identify a tree, a bird, or a squirrel is to begin to understand how the natural world is structured. But in order to identify something, you need to know *how* to see it. You need to know what to look for. Key characteristics that identify a plant or animal are called "field marks." A Beech Tree can be identified by its smooth gray bark; an American Redstart by the orange patches on its black wings and tail; a Golden-mantled Ground Squirrel by its bright rufous face and white side stripe. Color is an ideal key to begin unlocking nature's complexity.

I have had the good fortune to travel and visit firsthand all of the forests described in this book. The species illustrated are selected from my own experience. Most of the plants and animals included are common and easy to see. Some, though less common, are the "cream of the crop" of North American wildlife. Included are selected trees, wildflowers, birds, mammals, reptiles, amphibians, and even some insects and spiders. With this book as a guide you can learn what to look for in any forest in the continental U.S. By coloring the pictures you will learn how to pay attention to what you see. In short, you will develop a naturalist's eye for detail.

Enjoy this book at home or, better yet, take it with you outdoors. The colorful world of forests awaits you. Discover it.

Simple leaves:
American Beech

Compound leaves:
Shagbark Hickory

How to Use This Book

Coloring. Nature uses both brilliant and subtle colors. A male Scarlet Tanager is almost breathtaking when seen in bright sunlight — his scarlet feathers seem to glow. The challenge of coloring a Scarlet Tanager is to get a bright enough red. On the other hand, the fur of an Eastern Cottontail Rabbit is mostly soft brown, but with shades of gray, black, and rufous. The trick to accurately coloring a Cottontail is to blend several colors that produce the desired shades. Subtle shades occur throughout nature. Leaves are not simply green. Some are dark green, some yellow-green, some blue-green. Although this book can be used with crayons or water colors, colored pencils may be most satisfactory. Colored pencils will permit you to most easily produce delicate color mixtures, as well as tones ranging from very dark to light. With some practice, you can color based on your own observations of the plants and animals in the field.

Trees. One convenient thing about plants is that they don't run or fly away. By spending a few moments looking at the different parts of a tree it is usually possible to identify it.

Trees come in two basic kinds. One kind is called *broad-leaved* trees and the other is *needle-leaved* trees.

Broad-leaved trees have wide flat leaves. Oaks and maples are typical examples. The leaves may be simple or compound. A simple leaf consists of a *single blade* on a leaf stalk; a *compound* leaf consists of several *leaflets* from a single stalk. Beech leaves are simple, but hickory leaves are compound. In some trees, leaves grow *opposite* each other on twigs or a twig. In other trees, the leaves *alternate*. Most trees have alternate leaves, but some, such as maples, have opposite leaves. Leaves may be oval, heart-shaped, or elon-

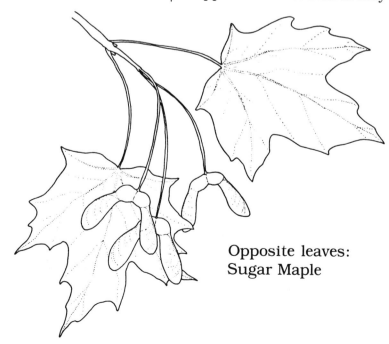

Opposite leaves:
Sugar Maple

gate. Some trees have leaves with small, sawlike *teeth* around the edge. Leaves may have *lobes*, which may be rounded or pointed. Some leaves feel leathery, some papery. Many broad-leaved trees are *deciduous*, which means that they drop their leaves in autumn and grow new leaves in spring. Some, however, are *evergreen* and keep their leaves throughout the year.

Broad-leaved trees produce *flowers*. Many trees bear small flowers that are hard to see and are not, therefore, useful as field marks. However, a few trees such as the Tulip Tree and Redbud are easily identified by their flowers. Petal color is important in identifying flowers; in many species *bracts* are important as well. Bracts are modified leaves that often resemble petals and grow from the flower base. Flowering Dogwood has prominent bracts.

Needle-leaved trees include the pines, spruces, firs, hemlocks, and junipers. With very few exceptions, all are evergreen. Needles may be stiff or soft, long or short. In pines, needles grow in clumps called *bundles*, and it is important to note the number of needles per bundle.

Needle-leaved trees are *conifers*, which means they do not have flowers but produce seeds in *cones*. Cones are usually brown and may feel prickly or smooth.

Bark color and texture are often useful field marks for both broad-leaved and needle-leaved trees. Bark may be scaly, furrowed, ridged, or smooth. It may peel off in strips, scales, or plates. It may be gray, reddish, or some other color.

Alternate leaves:
Yellow Birch

Oval leaves:
Live Oak

Hemlock

White Pine

Heartshaped, toothed leaves:
American Basswood

Elongated leaves:
Mountain Laurel

Lobed leaves:
Sassafras

Bract:
Flowering Dogwood

Wildflowers. Much of what was said about broad-leaved trees applies to identifying wildflowers. Color and shape of the flower are always important. Leaf characteristics are often important. Most forest wildflowers bloom in the spring. Many wildflowers are shown in *A Field Guide to the Wildflowers Coloring Book,* so only a few are included in this book.

Birds. Birds are conspicuous. They are often brightly colored, vocal, and active during the day. To identify birds, look for field marks such as size and shape of the bill, presence or absence of wing bars, wing patches, or a white rump. But above all, color is important. The bird descriptions in this book emphasize colors that serve as important field marks. In addition, some information is included on song and behavior as they help in identification. Birds are treated in *A Field Guide to the Birds Coloring Book.* However, many of the species included in this book are not illustrated in that volume.

Mammals. Mammals lack the bright colors of birds, but they are by no means dull. Their coat colors range from pure black or white to many shades of brown, gray, and rust. Important field marks include overall shape and size, characteristics of the tail (ringed, bushy, naked, short, or long), and the markings on the face. Mammals tend to be active at night and many are fairly secretive. Seeing them well is a challenge.

Other Animals. Reptiles and amphibians are very colorful. As you search the forests for turtles, snakes, frogs, and salamanders you will be pleasantly surprised at the bright colors of many species. This book includes some of the most colorful and abundant species. To see these reptiles and amphibians you may have to search under logs, rocks, and other hiding places.

Insects and spiders come in a wide variety of shapes and colors. It has been possible only to skim the surface in selecting species to include in this book. These interesting examples should whet your appetite to look more closely at the "little animals" of the forest.

It's time to begin. Open the pages and prepare to color. I hope your enjoyment in using this book matches mine in writing it.

John Kricher

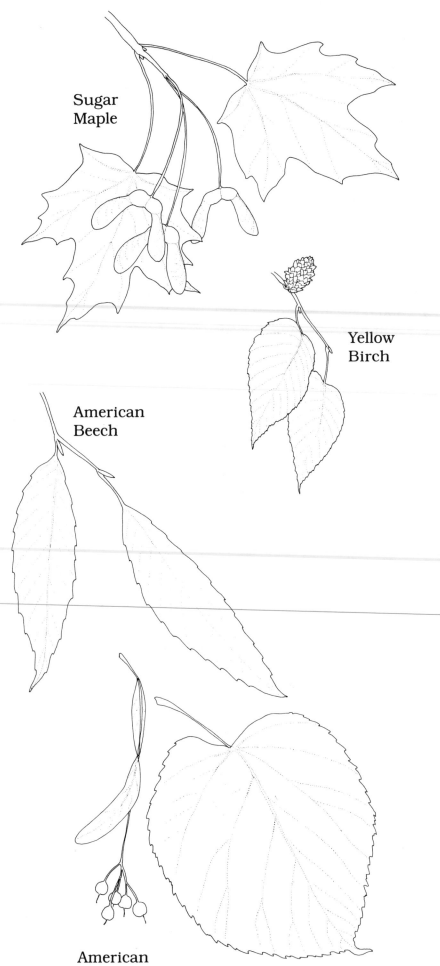

Sugar Maple

Yellow Birch

American Beech

American Basswood

The Northern Hardwoods Forest

This forest extends from northern New England to northern Minnesota. Trees that drop their leaves in the fall are the most common species, but evergreens such as Hemlock and White Pine are also common.

Sugar Maple (1) is an abundant species whose leaves turn from green to bright orange-red in fall. Like other maples, sugar maples have opposite leaves that are rounded with five pointed lobes. Maple seeds occur in pairs, on winged fruits.

Yellow Birch (2) leaves are oval in shape with tiny teeth along their edges. Bark is shiny yellowish and easily peels. Birch flowers are called catkins and hang from the twigs like small green cones. Both male and female catkins can grow on the same twig.

American Beech (3) is recognized by its very smooth, light gray bark. It has alternate leaves that are oval with large teeth along the edges. Leaves turn light brown in fall and feel very papery. They often hang on the tree for much of the winter.

American Basswood or Linden (4) has alternate heart-shaped leaves that are large, up to 5 inches long. Fruits are clusters of small yellowish berries that hang from slender, long, greenish yellow leaflike bracts.

Hemlock (5) is a conifer with cones less than an inch long that hang from the tips of the branches. The dark green needles are very short and flattened.

The **Eastern White Pine** (6) has soft yellow-green needles in bundles of five. Cones are long, up to 5 inches, with open scales. White pines can grow to 150 feet tall and are the tallest trees of the northern forests.

The **Jack Pine** (7) is a small pine that grows on dry sandy soils. The cones are brown and curve inward toward the branch. The dark green needles are short and stiff and come in bundles of two. Jack Pine cones only drop their seeds after being exposed to heat from a fire.

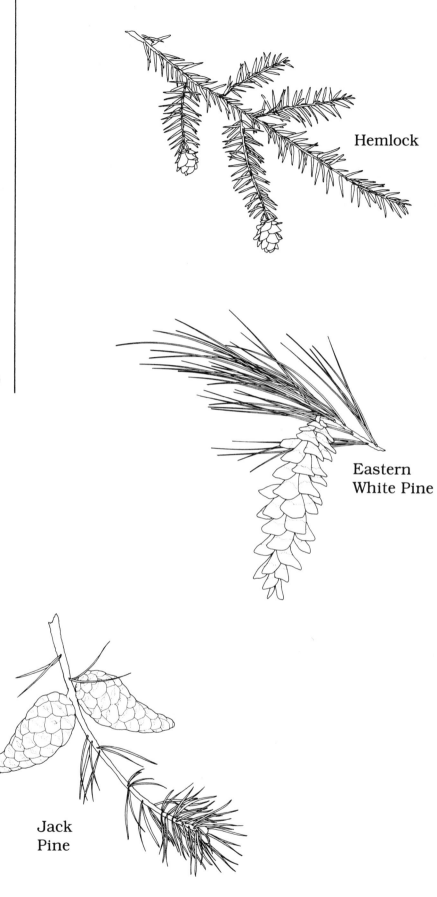

Hemlock

Eastern
White Pine

Jack
Pine

Forest Community Food Chain

In nature everything seems to serve as food for something else. Even the casual observer of the natural world will soon notice the impressive adaptations of predators for capturing prey and of prey for avoiding capture. Obviously, nature is organized in part by the rule of "eat or be eaten."

Where does the food come from? The answer is clear: from the sun. Ultimately, all food energy that passes through any living body, be it plant or animal, originated 93 million miles from earth in the sun. The sun's energy travels to earth as light.

Green plants have the chemical skills to convert sunlight into food. Using a green pigment called chlorophyll, plants make it possible for all other forms of life to exist. Plants form the first link in the ecological food chain. They are *producers*.

Animals are *consumers*. Many animals, from caterpillars to cottontails, eat only plants. These animals, called *herbivores*, form the second link in the food chain.

A caterpillar may be eaten by a shrew, or a cottontail by a weasel. Both the shrew and the weasel are *carnivores*. All carnivores are at least three links away from the sun on the food chain.

As an example, consider the illustration on the opposite page. The **Striped Maple** (8) is common in moist areas in the northern hardwoods forest. Its leaves are three-lobed and toothed and its young bark is green with white stripes. The maple is being fed upon by a **Green Looper caterpillar** (9). Loopers feed heavily on leaves before turning into adult moths. The **Black-capped Chickadee** (10), making a quick meal of the Looper, is identified by its black bib and cap, and gray body feathers.

Finally, the **Sharp-shinned Hawk** (11) prepares to try and capture the Chickadee for its meal. Sharp-shinned Hawks specialize in catching birds. They have a blue-gray body and wing feathers, a white breast with rusty barring, and a long, squarish, barred tail. Sharp-shins skulk in the trees, darting suddenly at their prey.

In this example of a food chain, the energy has gone from the sun to the Striped Maple, to the Green Looper, to the Black-capped Chickadee, to the Sharp-shinned Hawk. At each step, much of the original energy from the sun was used — by the maple leaf, the looper, the chickadee, and the hawk. The hawk got only what was "left over" after the others had used some. That's why there are so many fewer hawks than loopers.

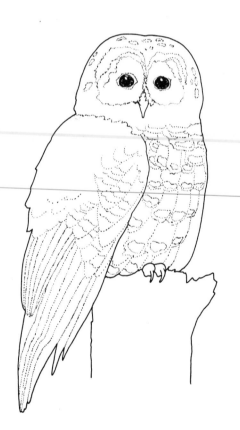

Sharp-shinned
Hawk

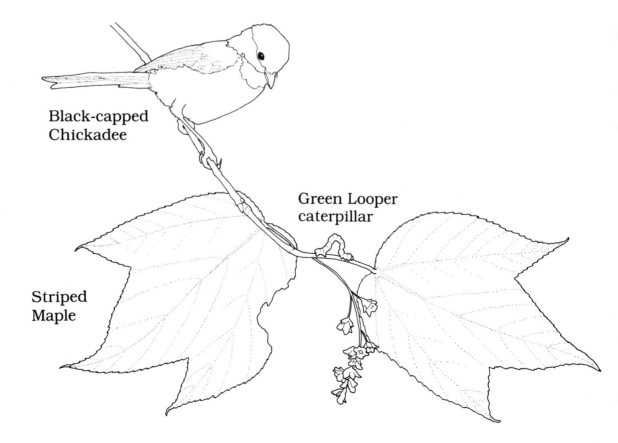

Black-capped
Chickadee

Green Looper
caterpillar

Striped
Maple

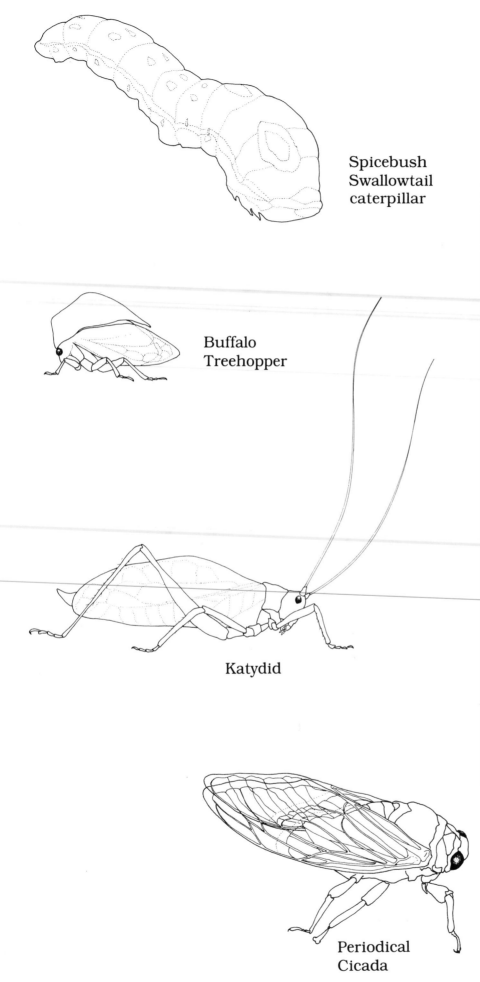

Spicebush
Swallowtail
caterpillar

Buffalo
Treehopper

Katydid

Periodical
Cicada

Plant-Eating Insects

Like all forests, the northern hardwoods forest has many insect species that thrive on a diet of leaves. The following are representative examples.

The caterpillar of the **Spicebush Swallowtail** (12) butterfly is one of the most remarkable looking of all caterpillars. Large and fleshy, it is emerald green above and yellowish-green on the sides. It has rows of small yellow dots along its length. The most striking field mark is the enlarged area toward the head, which has two large yellow spots with black spots inside. When viewed head-on, these spots look like large eyes, and they may give would-be predators the feeling that they are looking at a snake instead of a caterpillar.

The Buffalo Treehopper and Katydid both resemble green leaves. This camouflage helps protect them from predators. **Buffalo Treehoppers** (13) lay their eggs inside leaves, bark, and stems. They spend their entire lives in the leaves. **Katydids** (14) are closely related to grasshoppers. In late summer, males sound a rhythmic *katydid, katy-didn't* by rubbing their forewings together.

Cicadas are large insects usually found on bark. One species, the **Periodical Cicada** (15), spends from 13 to 17 years in the soil as a larva. Large numbers of adults then emerge at the same time and mate. They are metallic blue-green with red eyes and red wing veins.

Plant-eating Mammals

Rodents, rabbits and hares, and hoofed mammals have all adapted to a diet of nothing but plants. The animals below are found throughout wooded areas of the North and East.

Whitetail Deer (16) can be recognized by the prominent white patch visible under the tail as the animal bounds away. The body is buffy-brown with a white neck and belly. Only the males have antlers. Fawns are chestnut-colored with white speckles. Deer eat the twigs, buds, leaves, and bark of many broad-leaved plants.

Porcupines (17) are large rodents that eat the bark of many trees. They damage trees by gnawing deeply into the trunk. Their hair consists of large quills, which are mostly black but have white at the base. The stiff pointed quills protect these slow-moving animals from predators.

The **Beaver** (18) is the largest North American rodent, weighing up to 80 pounds. Like all rodents, beavers have pairs of large cutting teeth in their upper and lower jaws. Beavers cut down trees with their teeth, then use the trees to build large dams and lodges. They feed on both land and water plants. Their large paddle-like tails and webbed hind feet make Beavers excellent underwater swimmers.

The **White-footed Mouse** (19) has bulging black eyes, white feet and undersides, and warm brown fur on its upper sides and back. It feeds mostly on seeds and is the most abundant mammal of the forest.

Whitetailed Deer

Porcupine

Beaver

White-footed Mouse

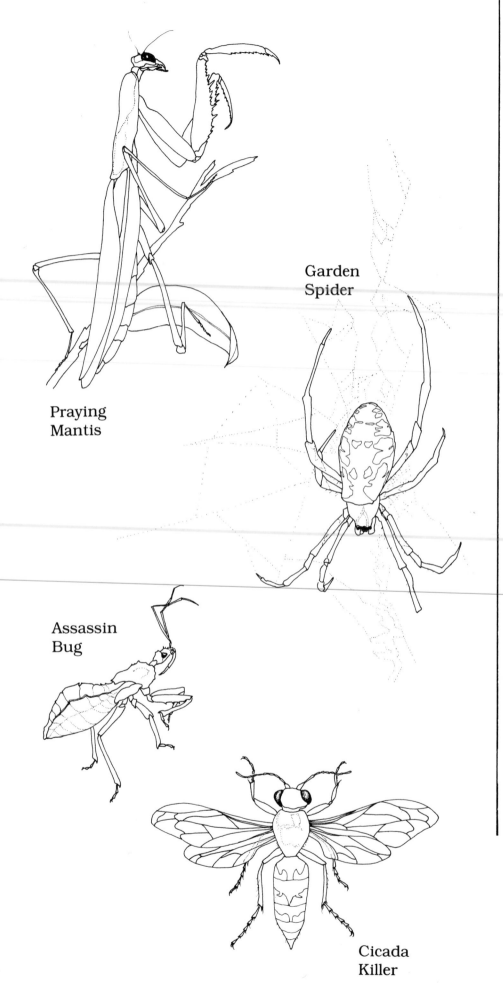

Praying
Mantis

Garden
Spider

Assassin
Bug

Cicada
Killer

Flesh-eating Arthropods

Insects and spiders are arthropods — animals that have their skeletons on the outside. Their legs, like ours, move at hinged joints. All forests have many species of arthropods. The following are among those most commonly seen in the northern hardwoods. All of them live by capturing and eating other animals.

The **Praying Mantis** (20) is a large slender insect that may be either brown or green, depending upon whether it is living on twigs or among leaves. Being well camouflaged, it is able to sneak up on and capture its insect prey. The Praying Mantis then quickly cuts its prey with the sharp, knifelike spines on its first pair of legs.

Assassin Bugs (21) are well hidden among flowers and leaves. These insects ambush their prey, piercing the body with their spearlike mouthparts and sucking out the juices. They are light yellowish brown.

The **Cicada Killer** (22) is a large (1½ inch) wasp, colored jet black with bright yellow bands. The female preys exclusively on cicadas. She stings and paralyzes them, then places them in her underground burrow with her eggs. When the larval wasp hatches, it feeds on the still-living cicada.

The **Garden Spider** (23) is common, not only in the northern hardwoods, but throughout the country. It lives in fields on the forest edge. The black and yellow female captures insects in the elaborate rounded web she weaves.

14

Flesh-eating Mammals

The northern hardwoods forest is the home of many mammalian predators.

The **Bobcat** (24) is not limited to the northern hardwoods but ranges throughout North American forests. Much larger than a domestic cat, a Bobcat weighs 20–30 pounds. The face is rounded; the ears are tufted with black tips. The short "bobbed tail" is a useful field mark. The bobcat is tawny with scattered black spots, especially along its sides. The underbelly is white. Bobcats feed on birds and mammals. Like most cats, they are good climbers.

The **Longtail Weasel** (25) is very common in the northern hardwoods, but can also be found throughout the U.S. The bright black eyes, slender shape, and furry black-tipped tail are good field marks. The body is rich rusty brown above and whitish yellow below. In northern states this weasel becomes uniformly white with a black tail tip in winter. It feeds on birds and mammals, which it kills by piercing the back of the skull.

The **Starnose Mole** (26) is a little black mammal with a pink ring of fleshy tentacles on its nose. It is common in the northern hardwoods. It lives underground, tunneling with its large front paws. Although its eyesight is very poor, it can locate worms and other food with its sensitive nose.

The **Shorttail Shrew** (27) is a slender, mouse-sized, shiny gray animal. Its pointed snout, tiny eyes, and lack of external ears help distinguish it from a mouse. Shrews have poison glands near their teeth which they use to kill insects and worms.

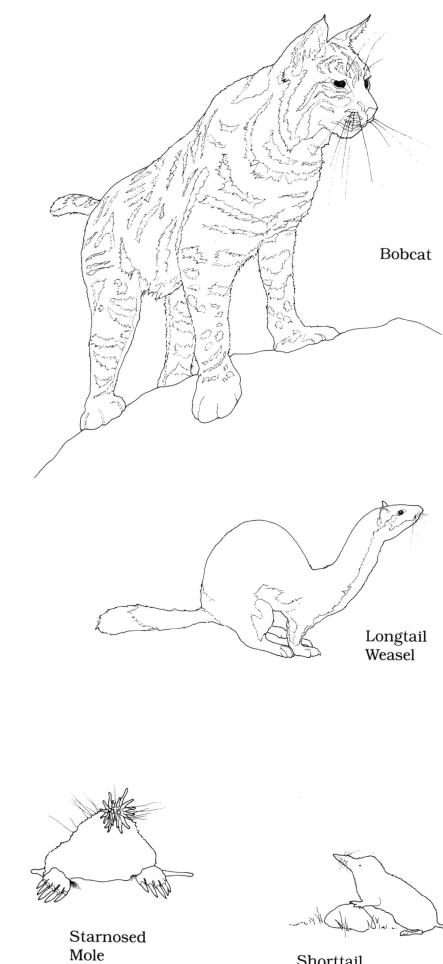

Bobcat

Longtail
Weasel

Starnosed
Mole

Shorttail
Shrew

Raccoon

Striped
Skunk

Gray Fox

Red Fox

Black Bear

Mammals That Eat Plants and Animals

Omnivore *is a term used for animals that feed on both plants and animals. Their diets often change as food sources vary with the seasons.*

The **Raccoon** (28) is a stocky animal that seems to shuffle along casually. Mostly seen at night, the Raccoon is identified by its black eye-mask and bushy tail with black rings. Its fur is dark brown, and its snout is sharply pointed. Raccoons feed on anything from fruit to fish; they often raid garbage cans.

The **Striped Skunk** (29) is easy to identify by its thick black fur with prominent white side stripes. The tail is very bushy with a white stripe on top. When in danger, skunks can squirt a foul-smelling oil at an enemy up to 10 feet away.

The Red and Gray Foxes are both common. The **Red Fox** (30) is uniform reddish brown above with a bushy white-tipped tail. The **Gray Fox** (31) is gray above with rufous on its sides only. Its tail is black on top and at the tip and is not as thick as the Red's. The Gray Fox is one of the few members of the dog family that sometimes climbs trees.

The **Black Bear** (32) is the only bear in the East. It is large and usually black with a small white chest patch that is usually hidden. Some western black bears are nearly cinnamon brown. Black Bears will eat almost anything and can become nuisances at garbage dumps and campgrounds. They can be dangerous if threatened.

Northern Hardwoods Birds

Most birds of northern forests are migrants, wintering in the southern states or the tropics. In spring they return and fill the woodlands with song.

The **Solitary Vireo** (33) sings its slow melodious whistle from the treetops. It has a blue-gray head with white spectacles around its eyes. Its back is greenish olive, and it has two wing bars on each wing.

The **Black-throated Blue Warbler** (34) male is easily identified by his black throat and blue head and back. His song is buzzy and insectlike, rising in pitch.

The **Rose-breasted Grosbeak** (35) is usually spotted singing its robinlike song about 20 feet up in a tree. Male has a rosy red breast, large white wing patches, and a white rump. The head, back, wings, and tail are black. The large thick bill is white. Females are brown-streaked and resemble over-grown sparrows.

Many consider the flutelike song of the **Hermit Thrush** (36) to be the richest of all bird songs. The Hermit Thrush is brown with a rusty tail. Its breast is white with black spots. It hops like a robin.

The **Ruffed Grouse** (37) is a large chickenlike bird, most easily identified by its fan-shaped tail, which may be rufous or gray. Its body is rich brown with black bars. Displaying birds fluff out their black neck ruffs, giving the bird its name.

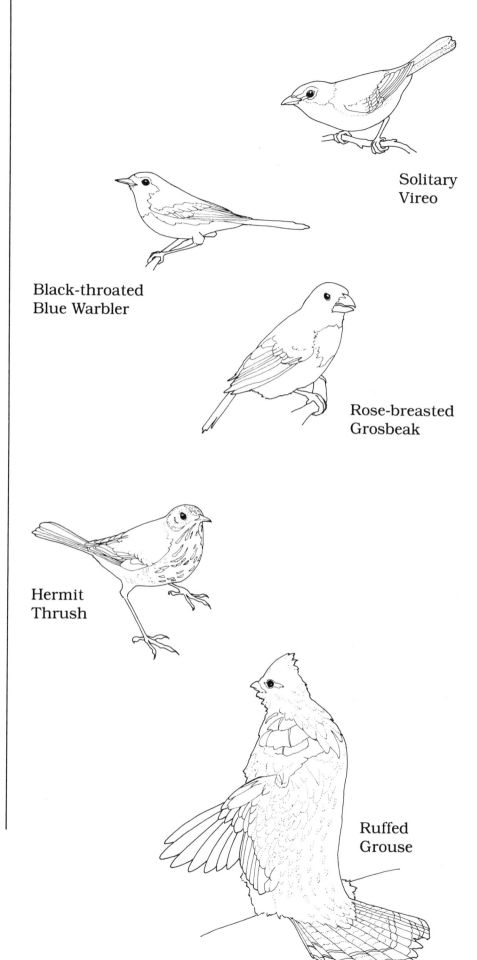

Solitary Vireo

Black-throated Blue Warbler

Rose-breasted Grosbeak

Hermit Thrush

Ruffed Grouse

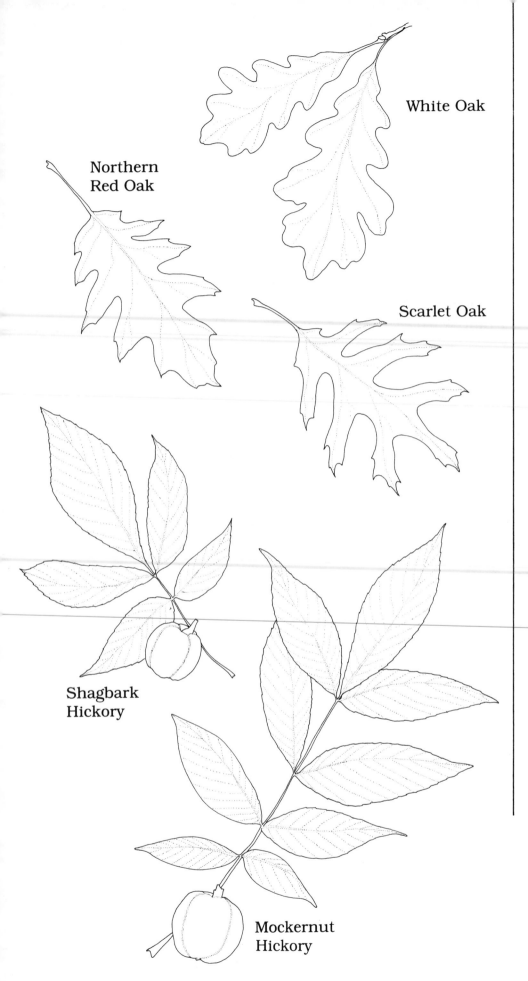

White Oak

Northern
Red Oak

Scarlet Oak

Shagbark
Hickory

Mockernut
Hickory

Oak-Hickory Forest

Ranging from New England to Texas, the Gulf Coast to Minnesota, the oak-hickory forest covers a tremendous area. In most places it has grown back on land that has been farmed or logged; this is termed second-growth forest. The oak-hickory forest is characterized by trees that produce nuts, such as acorns, hickory nuts, and, until this century, chestnuts. Oaks of many species are common. All oaks have alternate leaves; many have lobed leaves.

White Oak (38) leaves vary in shape, but always have 7–9 rounded lobes. They are bright green and turn brownish in fall. Bark is grayish and peels in small scales.

Northern Red Oak (39) leaves have 7–11 lobes and each is sharply pointed. They turn deep red in fall. Bark is furrowed with alternate black and gray lines. **Scarlet Oak** (40) leaves are similar but more deeply lobed, and turn brilliant scarlet in fall.

Hickories have alternate leaves; each leaf is compound, divided into 5–9 oval leaflets, depending on the species. Leaves become yellow in fall. **Shagbark Hickory** (41) has bark that peels off in long strips. Leaves have five wide leaflets. Nuts grow inside thick-skinned green fruits. **Mockernut Hickory** (42) leaves have nine narrow leaflets and the bark doesn't peel. Nut is in a thick brown husk.

Other Common Trees

Flowering Dogwood (43) is an understory species, rarely growing over 30 feet tall. Its bright white blossoms, which appear in spring, consist of tiny red and yellow flowers surrounded by four petal-like bracts. The white bracts attract insects, which spread the pollen. Fruits are fleshy red berries. Leaves are opposite, oval, with prominent veins. Bark resembles alligator hide.

American Elm (44) is known for its tall, straight trunk and graceful symmetrical crown. Its alternate light green leaves are double-toothed and uneven at the base. Seeds are flat, encased in a notched wing. Many elms have been killed by Dutch Elm disease, a blight spread by bark beetles.

Black Locust (45) is most common along forest edges. In spring, clusters of cream-colored flowers hang from the tree. Seeds mature in 4-inch brown pods, like peas. Leaves are dark-green, large, alternate, and compound, with up to 21 oval leaflets. Twigs are thorny; the bark deeply ridged.

Red Maple (46) is abundant, growing in all habitats from swamps to mountainsides. Its small red flowers open in spring before it leafs out. Bark is very gray. Opposite leaves have three prominent upper lobes and two small basal lobes. Leaves are bright crimson in autumn. Seeds are on reddish wings.

Sweet Gum (47) is identified by its alternate yellow-green star-shaped leaves with five very sharply pointed lobes. Seeds are held in prickly balls that hang from the branches.

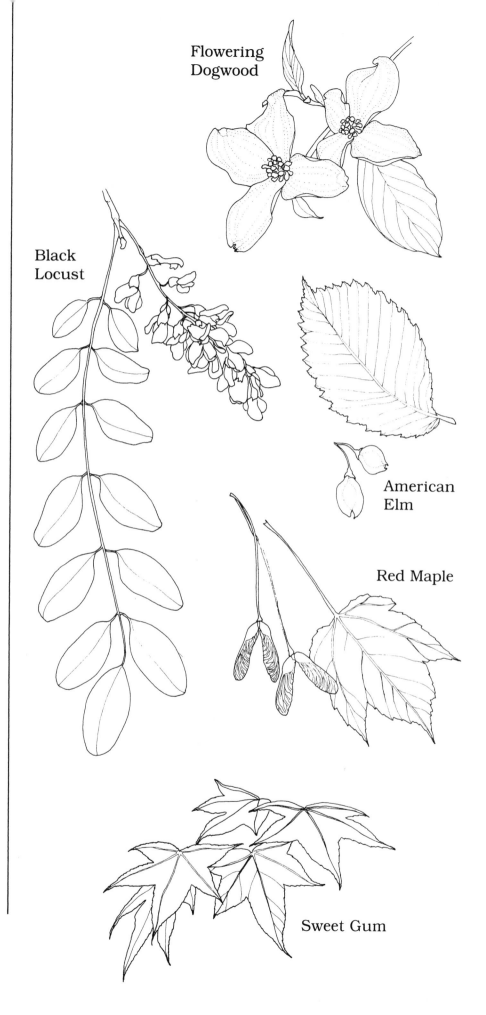

Flowering Dogwood

Black Locust

American Elm

Red Maple

Sweet Gum

19

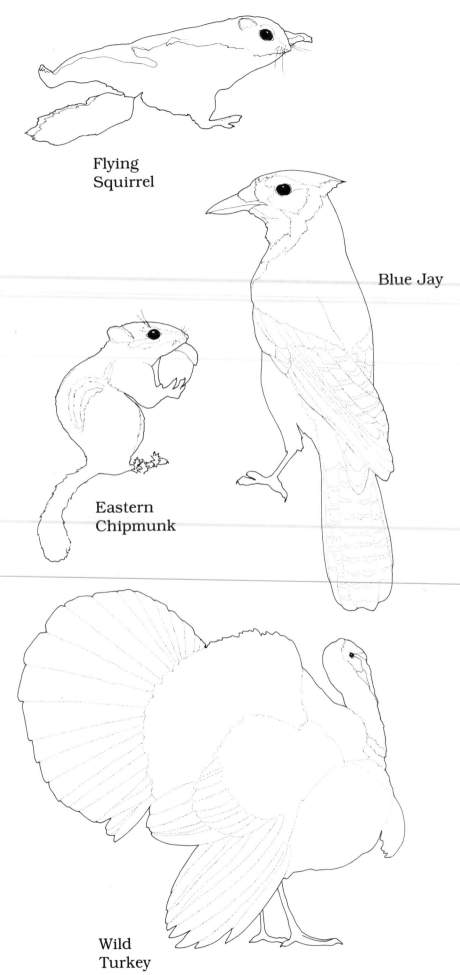

Flying
Squirrel

Blue Jay

Eastern
Chipmunk

Wild
Turkey

Nut-eaters

Flying Squirrels (48) though abundant, come out only well after dark, so they are rarely seen. The wide skin flaps connecting the legs allow them to glide (not fly) between trees. The back and head are a warm brown color. The body and flattened tail are white underneath. Eyes are large and black. Flying Squirrels nest inside tree cavities.

Eastern Gray Squirrels (48a; shown on title page) are probably the best known consumers of nuts. They are quite grayish, with bushy, blackish gray tails and pale white underbellies.

The Eastern Chipmunk (49) is a small ground squirrel. It is chestnut with a white face and black-and-white side stripes. When disturbed, it emits a sharp, birdlike squeak. Chipmunks nest in underground burrows or within stone walls. They hibernate in winter.

The **Blue Jay** (50) is a common and conspicuous bird. It is identified by its large size, prominent crest, and black necklace. It's the only blue and white bird with a crest. Jays make many sounds, but are usually heard scolding *jay jay*. They are partially migratory; their local abundance varies with the size of the acorn crop.

Wild Turkeys (51) differ from barnyard turkeys in having rusty tail tips (white in barnyard turkeys), and more slender bodies. Feathers are shiny bronze. The head is bluish with red wattles. Surprisingly secretive, the gobbler male is rarely observed in full display before the hens.

Bats

Bats occur in all forests, but the species on this page are found only in the East. Bats are the only flying mammals. Appearing at dusk, they fly in pursuit of insects throughout the night. Bat wings are bare skin supported by long finger bones. Their eyesight is poor, but bats have evolved a remarkable radar system to locate prey. As a bat flies, it emits a very high-pitched sound that bounces off objects and returns, to be received by the bat's large ears. Using this radar, a bat can both avoid obstacles and locate flying insects. Because of their rapid flight and nighttime hours, bats are difficult to identify in the field.

The **Little Brown Bat** (52) is abundant. It is small, uniformly brown, with medium-sized ears. It roosts in attics, barns, and hollow trees. In winter thousands gather in caves to hibernate.

The **Eastern Pipistrel** (53) is identified by its small size, light brown fur, and weak butterfly-like flight. One of the smallest bats, it hibernates deep in caves.

Both the **Red Bat** (54) and **Hoary Bat** (55) are large, with wide wingspreads. Both are migratory, moving south for the winter. Red Bats are bright rusty, almost the color of a red fox. Solitary individuals often roost low in shrubs. Hoary Bats have a white frosted look.

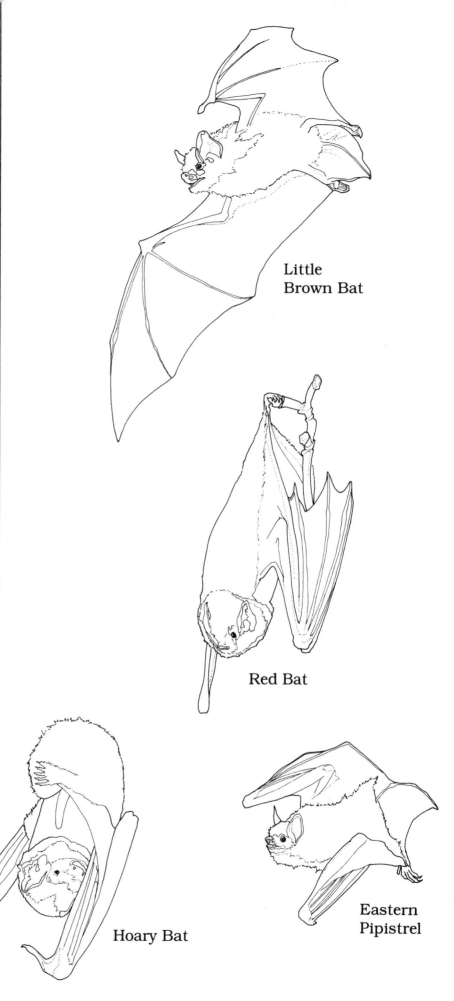

Little Brown Bat

Red Bat

Hoary Bat

Eastern Pipistrel

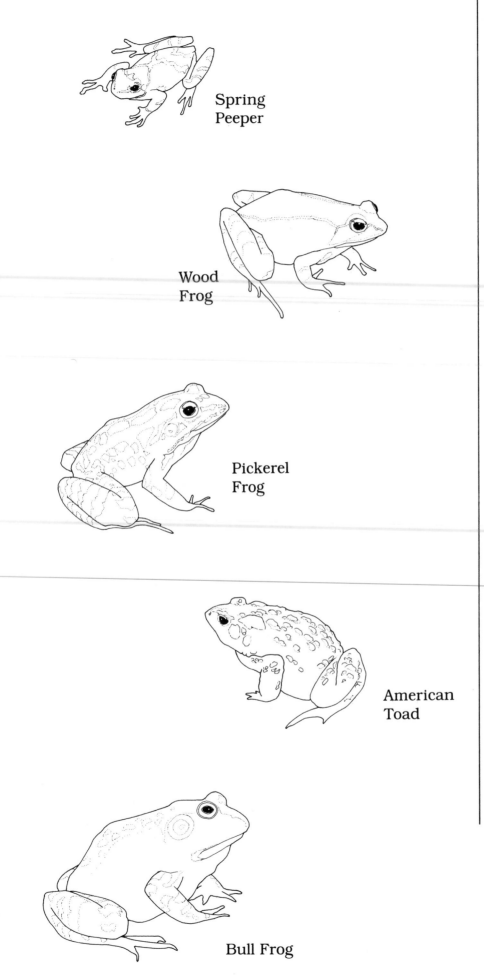

Spring
Peeper

Wood
Frog

Pickerel
Frog

American
Toad

Bull Frog

Frogs and Toads

Spring is the season to see frogs and toads in eastern woodlands. They gather at ponds calling, mating, and laying eggs. Soon small aquatic tadpoles hatch and develop into adult frogs and toads. As adults, frogs and toads feed on insects they spear with their long sticky tongues.

Spring Peepers (56) begin calling very early in spring. Their steady high-pitched *peep peep* is heard in all eastern states. Only 1 inch long, Peepers are tan with a dark brown *x* on the back. The Peeper is a tree frog — each toe ends in a small suction disc, which they use to cling to grass and stems.

Wood Frogs (57) also breed in early spring. Their mating call is a duck-like quacking, often heard throughout the day. Inhabitants of the forest floor, they are light brown with a dark patch behind the eye.

Pickerel Frogs (58) are gray-brown, heavily spotted with dark brown. Also called "grass frogs," they are frequently seen in wet meadows as well as ponds and streams. Their voice, a low wheeze, does not carry far.

American Toads (59) emit a loud steady trill. Toads have dry warty skin and move in short hops, not leaps. The skin is light brown and warts are dark brown.

The 8-inch **Bull Frog** (60) is a champion jumper. It is the largest green frog. Its call is a low twangy *jug-rum.*

Eastern Forest Reptiles

Turtles, snakes, and lizards are reptiles. Their skins are cool, dry, and covered with scales. Their toes have claws. The following reptiles are common throughout eastern forests.

The **Eastern Box Turtle** (61) is identified by its high-domed brown shell, liberally splotched with yellow-orange. Its legs and head are black with yellow spots. Males have red eyes, females brown eyes. When in danger it closes its hinged shell, completely covering its head.

The **Wood Turtle** (62) can be found in wet meadows or dry woods. It is orange on its throat, neck, and legs. The brown shell is somewhat flattened and displays an intricate pattern of shields with radiating ridges.

The **Eastern Hognose Snake** (63) has an upturned snout and yellow chin. Its body is yellowish brown with dark brown blotches. When threatened, it will hiss and puff out its head like a cobra. Should this tactic fail, it will turn over and play dead.

The **Eastern Milk Snake** (64) is white with dark red blotches bordered by black. Both the hognose and milk snakes are non-poisonous.

The **Timber Rattlesnake** (65) is poisonous. Its head is large and triangular. It is light brown with dark brown bands bordered by yellow. It is not common, *but be extremely careful if you encounter one.*

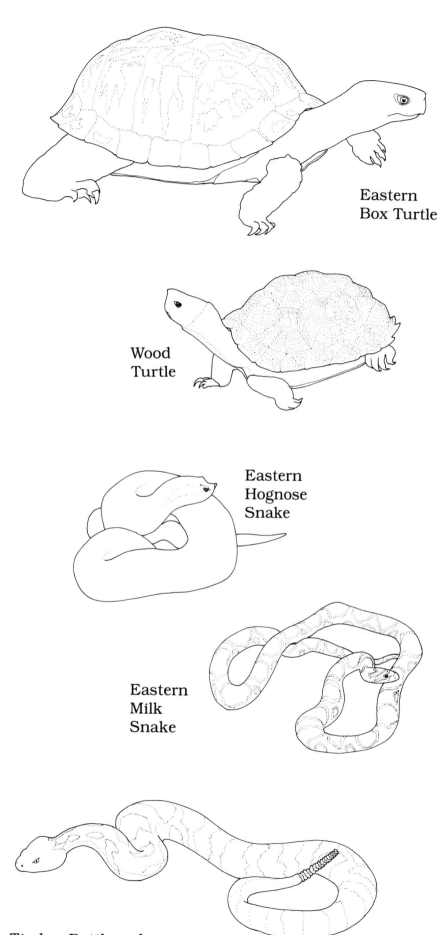

Eastern
Box Turtle

Wood
Turtle

Eastern
Hognose
Snake

Eastern
Milk
Snake

Timber Rattlesnake

Isopod

Carrion
Beetle

Centipede

False
Scorpion

Soil
Mite

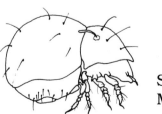

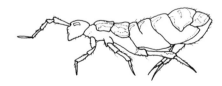
Springtail

Animals of the Soil

In all forests, decaying leaves and animal bodies supply food for many tiny animals. The variety of animals living in the forest litter is easily observed with only a hand lens or magnifying glass.

Isopods (66) or Sowbugs are uniformly gray. They can roll tightly into a ball when in danger. Common under logs and rocks.

Carrion Beetles (67) are large black insects with prominent red spotting. When several carrion beetles discover a small dead animal such as a mouse, they bury it.

Centipedes (68) are wormlike, with many body segments and long thin legs. Most are dark brown. Their heads are armed with strong jaws, and they can move quickly to capture small insects.

False Scorpions (69) look like tiny scorpions with large crab-like claws. They are shiny orange-brown.

Soil Mites (70) have eight legs and resemble tiny spiders. Their color ranges from white to dark brown.

Springtails (71) are pale gray wingless insects. Their oddly structured abdomen helps them jump well. Large groups of Springtails sometimes appear on snow.

Insects Living in Wood

In all forests there are insects that are able to burrow into and survive inside wood. The following are among the most common.

Termites live in huge societies of workers, soldiers, and queen. They invade and eat wood. They digest the wood with the help of one-celled **Termite Gut Protozoans** (72) that live in their guts. Without the proto- zoans, a **Termite** (73) could not digest its diet of wood and would starve. The workers are all white, but the soldiers and queens are black with white ab- domens. Termites and ants are often confused, but they are easy to tell apart. All ant spe- cies are "pinched in" at the waist; termites are not.

Black Carpenter Ants (74) also live in huge societies inside old decaying trees or occasionally in wood houses. All are uni- formly glossy black. They feed on insects and fruits.

Bark Beetles (75) are blackish brown, small, and stocky, with enlarged tips on their short, club-shaped antennae. They at- tack both live and dead trees, laying eggs under the bark. Larvae make extensive tunnels (76).

Long-horned beetles such as the **Elm Borer** (77) lay eggs in wood and the larvae damage the tree. The colorful Elm Borer is blue-gray with orange-red markings. It has a slender body with very long antennae.

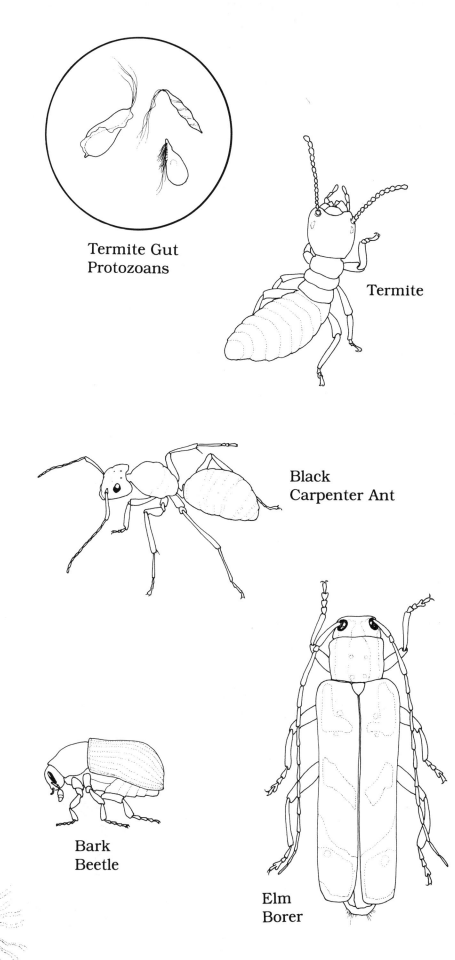

Termite Gut
Protozoans

Termite

Black
Carpenter Ant

Bark
Beetle

Elm
Borer

Bark Beetle
tunnels

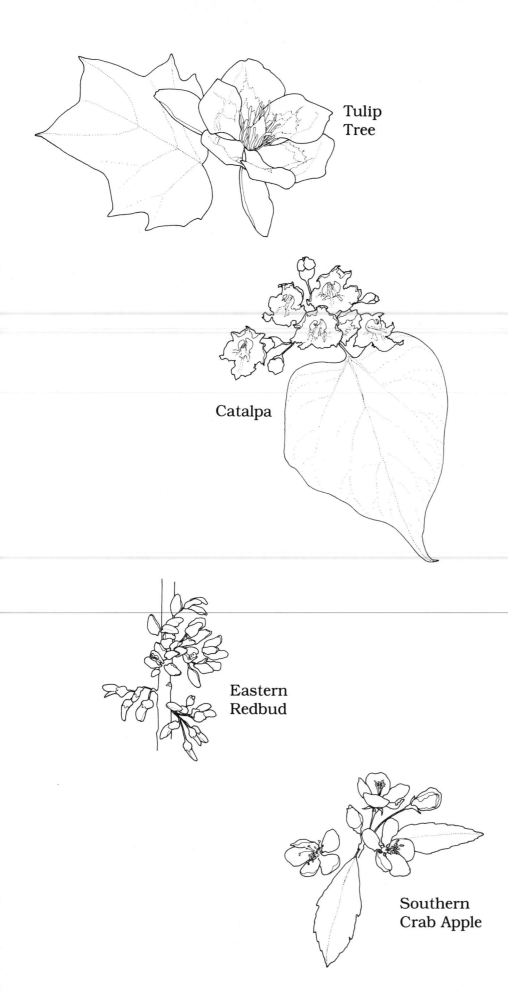

Tulip Tree

Catalpa

Eastern Redbud

Southern Crab Apple

Southern Appalachian Forest

The Great Smoky Mountains form the center of a vast forest that covers the inland areas of the Southeast. Over 100 tree species are found in the rich moist woodlands.

The **Tulip Tree** (78) is noted for its straight grayish trunk (up to 150 feet tall) and tuliplike blossoms. The flowers have six large petals, greenish yellow with orange at the base. Leaves are bright green, up to 10 inches wide, alternate, with four lobes.

Catalpa (79) belongs to a family of largely tropical trees. Clusters of delicate white flowers with purple and yellow dots grow at the branch tips. Large heart-shaped leaves are bright green. Seeds grow in 20-inch-long, slender, brown pods that hang from the branches after the leaves have fallen.

Eastern Redbud (80) has bright pink flower clusters that cover the tree before the broad heart-shaped leaves appear in spring. Redbuds have a wide crown and rarely grow above 50 feet. Seeds grow in brown pods.

Southern Crab Apple (81) is also a small tree. In spring clusters of five-petaled pink flowers appear on branch tips. Fruits are small, dark green apples. Leaves are oval and toothed.

Understory Trees and Shrubs

Sassafras (82) is abundant in the forest understory. It has leaves with three distinct shapes: unlobed, single-lobed, or double-lobed. Bark is deeply ridged. Fruits are small blue berries. Bark and roots are boiled to make tea.

Mountain Laurel, Flame Azalea, and Catawba Rhododendron are members of the heath family and grow well in acid soil.

Mountain Laurel (83) is a common thicket shrub. Its narrow, lance-shaped, evergreen leaves are dark green, thick, and waxy. Pinkish white flowers grow in dense clusters.

Flame Azalea (84) drops its leaves in winter. Leaves are elongate and oval; has clusters of tubular, vivid orange-red flowers. Favors mountainsides.

Catawba Rhododendron (85) is also called Mountain Rosebay. It has large pinkish red blossoms in dense clusters. Each flower is deep, like a funnel, with long yellow-tipped stamens. Leaves are evergreen, dark green above, light below, and very leathery. Prefers slopes.

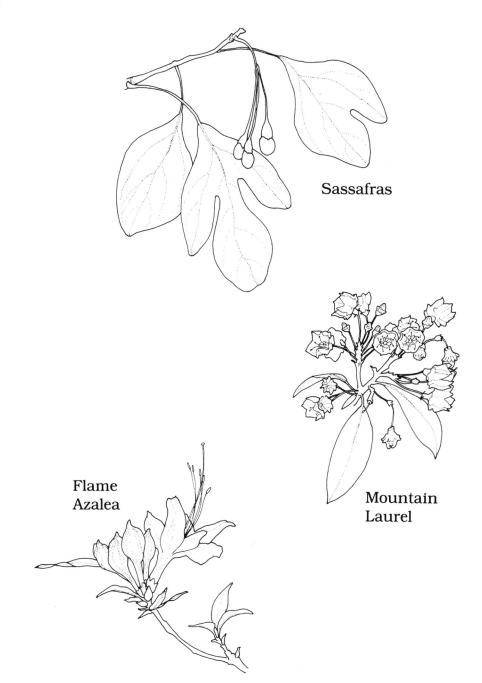

Sassafras

Flame Azalea

Mountain Laurel

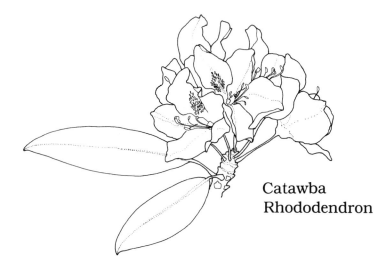

Catawba Rhododendron

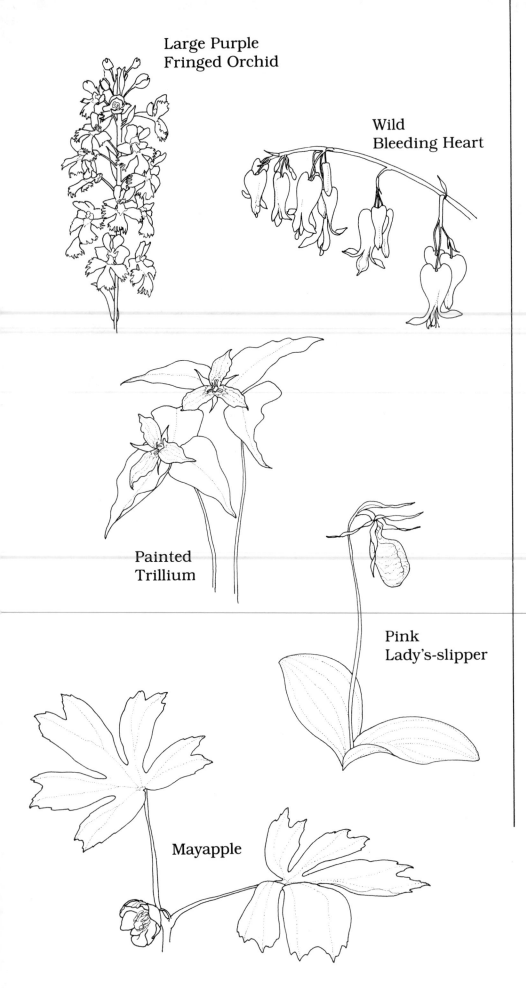

Large Purple
Fringed Orchid

Wild
Bleeding Heart

Painted
Trillium

Pink
Lady's-slipper

Mayapple

Forest Wildflowers

Cool forest shade and damp soils provide an excellent habitat for many kinds of wildflowers. The following are found not only in the Appalachians but in many other forests.

Large Purple Fringed Orchid (86) has many lavender flowers together on a long spike. The central lip petal, which leads insects to the nectar tube, consists of three delicately fringed lobes.

Wild Bleeding Heart (87) produces its clusters of dangling, heart-shaped, pinkish red flowers throughout the summer. Pale green leaves are deeply cut. Prefers rocky areas and slopes.

Painted Trillium (88) is named for its three, distinct, white petals, which become pinkish red at the base. The heart-shaped, dark green leaves also occur in threes. Flowers turn into bright red berries by late summer.

Pink Lady's-slipper (89) (Moccasin-flower) usually bears a single large flower with an inflated pink lip petal lined with deep red veins. Leaves are in twos, oval with distinct parallel veins. Leaves lie flat on the ground.

Mayapple (90) may carpet almost an entire forest floor in spring. Its foot-long, yellow-green, umbrella-like leaves are deeply lobed. Under the leaves is a single, large, white flower with a yellow center, growing on a nodding stem. Flowers in spring.

Mushrooms and Brackets

All forests host many species of these odd plants, none of which makes its own food as green plants do. Fungi send out networks of underground strands that take energy from dead leaves, twigs, and animals. Periodically, fungi grow colorful reproductive bodies called mushrooms and brackets. Mushrooms and brackets can spring up overnight from the ground or dead trees.

The **Chanterelle Mushroom** (91) is a rich buffy-orange, and has a collar or frill around its edge. This species is edible, but is easily confused with several poisonous species. *Never eat a mushroom unless you are certain of its identity.*

The poisonous **Fly Amanita** (92) is easy to recognize by its orange-red cap with white warts. The white stalk has a frill near the base of the cap.

Polypores (93) are a group of related species of bracket fungi. They are rich brown, and grow in overlapping shelves with bands of color.

Yellow Coral (94) has many upright yellow branches.

Turkeytail (95) is large and a colorful bright orange.

Chanterelle Mushroom

Fly Amanita

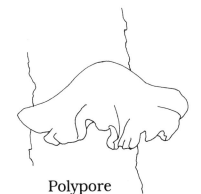

Polypore

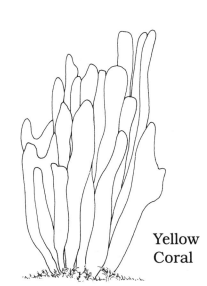

Yellow Coral

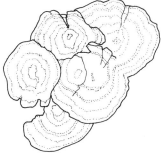

Turkeytail

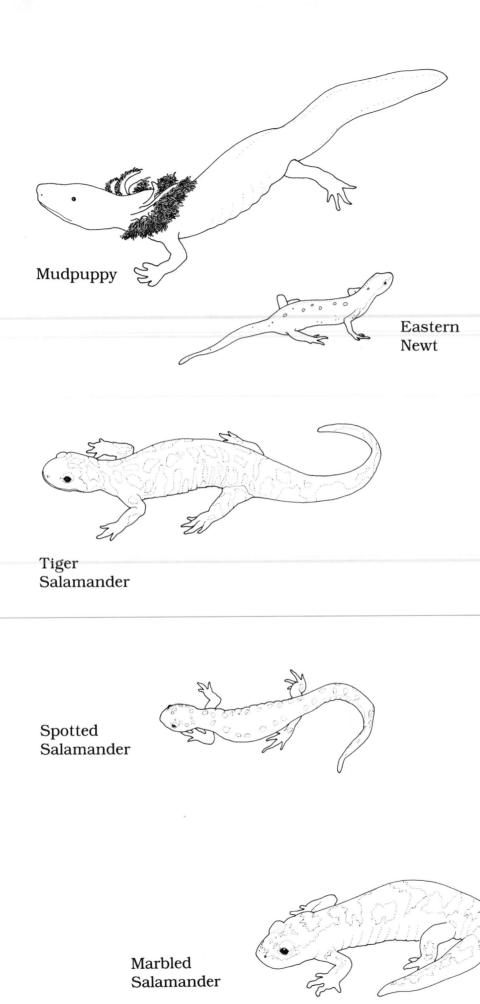

Mudpuppy

Eastern
Newt

Tiger
Salamander

Spotted
Salamander

Marbled
Salamander

Salamanders

The Appalachian Forest has more species of salamanders than anywhere else in the U.S. Salamanders, along with frogs and toads, are amphibians. Amphibians lack scales and claws and have moist skins. All salamanders feed on worms and small insects. Salamanders lay eggs in water. Their larvae live in water and breathe through featherlike gills on their necks.

The **Mudpuppy** (96) or Waterdog is unusual in that it retains its orange external gills as an adult. This 15-inch inhabitant of streams is rusty brown above with black blotches. Its underbelly is orange-red. Its tail has fins on its upper and lower side.

The **Eastern Newt** (97) is olive-green above with tiny red spots along its sides. Its underbelly is yellow. Juvenile newts are called Red Efts because of their salmon red color. They live on the forest floor.

The **Tiger Salamander** (98) is the largest land salamander, reaching lengths of over 1 foot. Its yellow underbelly and black body with yellow blotches give it its name. Found under moist logs.

The **Spotted Salamander** (99) is black above with scattered yellow dots. Its underbelly is gray. Following the first spring rains, masses migrate to breeding ponds. Found in leaf litter and under logs.

The **Marbled Salamander** (100) is black above with silvery interconnected lines. Its belly is black. Found under rocks.

Woodland and Streamside Salamanders

The **Red-backed Salamander** (101) is common in decaying logs. Two color phases exist. The red-backed phase is gray with a broad orange-red line from head to tail. The lead-backed phase is gray with pepperlike speckles.

The **Slimy Salamander** (102) closely resembles the lead-backed phase of the Red-backed Salamander, and is found in similar habitats. It is well-named, however, and can be reliably identified by its sticky, mucuslike skin.

The **Red-cheeked** or **Jordan's Salamander** (103) has a limited range, occurring only in the Great Smoky Mountains. Its color varies. Most common with uniform black above, grayish underbelly, and bright red-orange cheeks.

The **Long-tailed Salamander** (104) is found under rocks and wet logs. Its best field mark is its long tail. It is uniformly pale orange, speckled with black.

The **Red Salamander** (105) ranks among the most brilliantly colored salamanders. It lives in cool running streams and is the only salamander that is deep red with black dots.

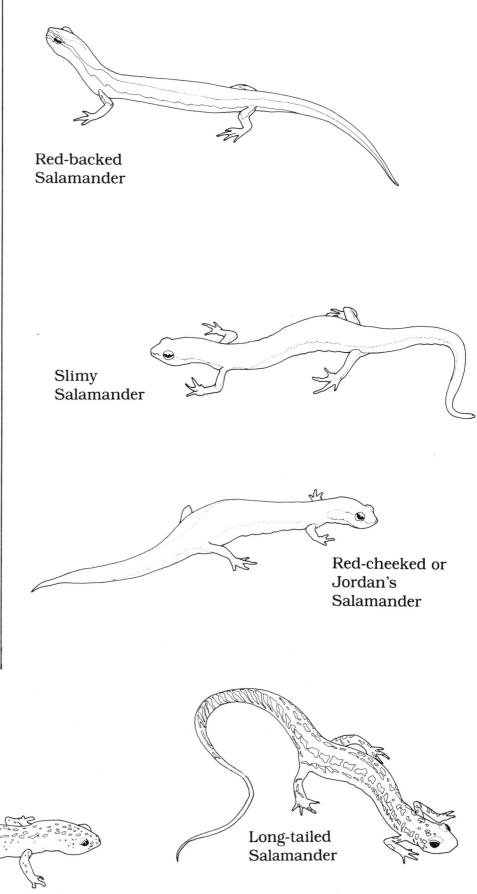

Red-backed
Salamander

Slimy
Salamander

Red-cheeked or
Jordan's
Salamander

Long-tailed
Salamander

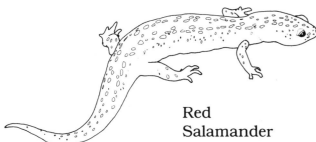

Red
Salamander

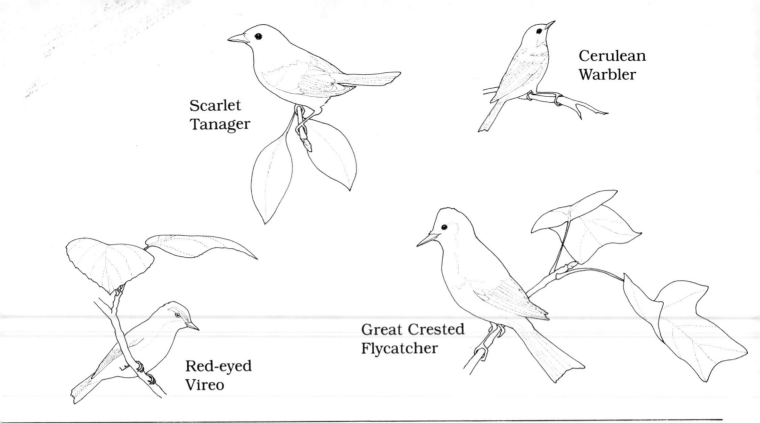

Scarlet Tanager

Cerulean Warbler

Red-eyed Vireo

Great Crested Flycatcher

Appalachian Forest Birds

In summer many different birds live in the Appalachian forest. The ones shown below all feed on insects. Since they feed in different parts of the forest they do not compete with one another.

In the tall trees are the Scarlet Tanager, Red-eyed Vireo, Cerulean Warbler, and Great Crested Flycatcher. The male **Scarlet Tanager** (106) is unmistakable with his scarlet body and black wings and tail. The constant warble of the **Red-eyed Vireo** (107) directs the birder's attention to an olive-green bird with a sharp white eye line, and red eyes. This vireo has a gray cap and lacks wing bars. As it searches for insects it moves slowly from branch to branch. The **Cerulean Warbler** (108) is blue and white, with white wing bars, a black necklace, and black side streaking. The bird typically feeds high in the treetops.

The **Great Crested Flycatcher** (109) often perches in the open.

It has a yellow breast, gray face and throat, and reddish brown tail. It darts from its perch to capture flying insects on the wing.

Below the forest canopy the Acadian Flycatcher, American Redstart, and Tufted Titmouse search for food. The drab brown **Acadian Flycatcher** (110) is identified by its small size, upright posture, wing bars, and white eye-ring. The **American Redstart** (111) flits from one tree to the next with its wings and tail spread, showing the bright orange patches on the black feathers. The **Tufted Titmouse** (112) is a small, crested, blue-gray bird. Its whistled *peter, peter* is easy to recognize.

The White-breasted Nuthatch and Black-and-white Warbler are specialists, probing the trunks and bark for insects and spiders. The **White-breasted Nuthatch** (113) has a blue back, white breast, and black cap. It moves upside down on the tree trunk. The **Black-and-white Warbler** (114) looks like a feathered zebra.

In the undergrowth are found the Worm-eating Warbler, Hooded Warbler, and Carolina Wren. The light brown **Worm-eating Warbler** (115) is identified by its black head stripes. It prefers hillsides where rhododendron growth is thick. The brilliant **Hooded Warbler** (116) has a bright yellow face and breast offset by a black hood. Its back and tail are olive-green. Its white tail patches are good field marks as it flies away. The bright rusty **Carolina Wren** (117) has a white stripe above its eyes. Its belly is light buffy. It calls *cheedala cheedala cheedala.*

The Ovenbird and Wood Thrush inhabit the forest floor. The small **Ovenbird** (118) calls *teacher, teacher;* the **Wood Thrush** (119) sings a melodious flutelike trill. Both birds have speckled breasts but the thrush is larger and is brown with a rufous head. The Ovenbird is olive-green, with a dull orange cap and white eye ring. The Thrush hops, and the Ovenbird walks.

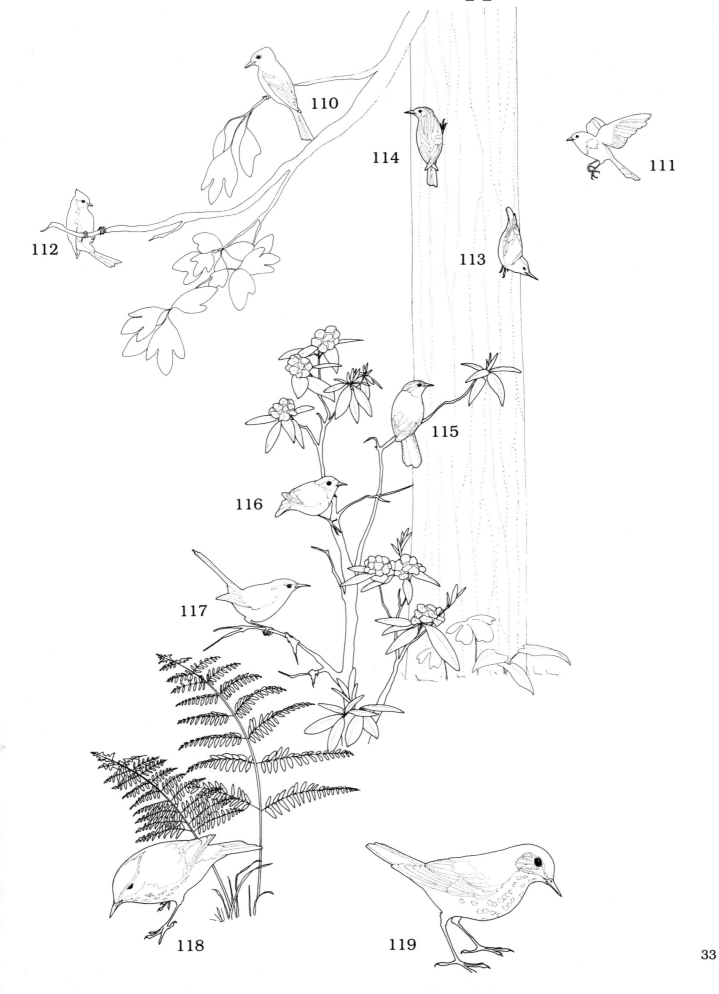

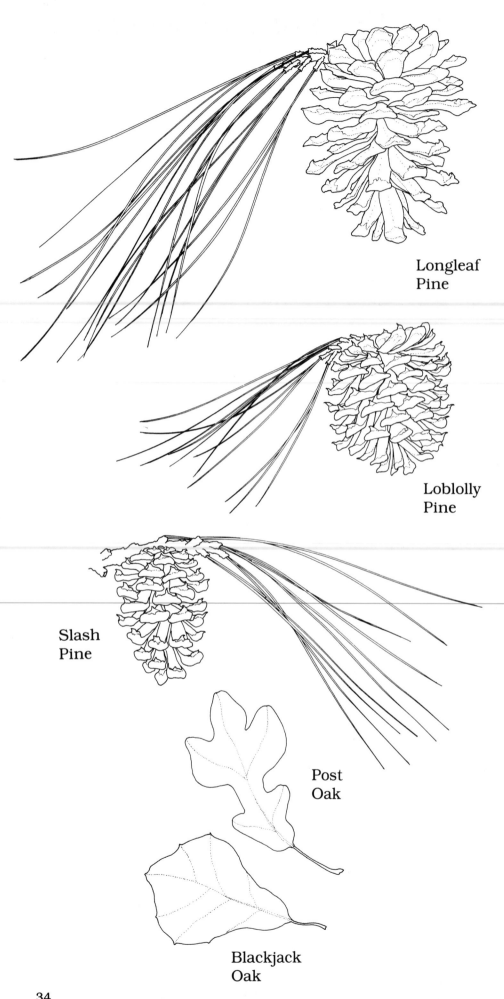

Longleaf
Pine

Loblolly
Pine

Slash
Pine

Post
Oak

Blackjack
Oak

Coastal Plain Forest

On dry sandy soils from the dunes of Cape Cod south along the East Coast to Florida and the Gulf States is a forest of pine and oak. Since the forest is dry, lightning-set fires are common in the summer months, and many of the trees show fire damage such as blackened trunks.

Longleaf Pine (120) needles are bright bluish green, grow to 18 inches in length, and are in bundles of three. The rusty-colored, prickly cones grow up to 10 inches long. The orange-brown bark has scaly plates. The seedlings are covered by a dense protective umbrella of thick needles that make them appear hairy and protect them from ground fires.

Loblolly Pine (121) has yellowish green needles up to 9 inches long in bundles of three. Reddish brown cones are prickly.

Slash Pine (122) resembles Loblolly but its 10-inch, dark green needles grow in bundles of two. Shiny brown cones are prickly. Bark is very reddish with many purplish scales.

Post Oak (23) grows abundantly on the coastal plain. Its deeply lobed, dark green leaves are shiny and feel leathery. The lobes are smoothly rounded.

Blackjack Oak (124) leaves are shiny yellow-green above, yellow below. Leaves are wide with sharp points at the tips of the veins. They vary in shape, but usually have three lobes. Leaves feel thick and leathery.

Birds of Coastal Plain Forests

The constant trill of the **Pine Warbler** (125) is often heard before the small bird is spotted. This warbler searches the pine needles for insects. It has a bright yellow breast and two white wing bars. Its back is olive-green.

The **Yellow-throated Warbler** (126) creeps about, searching for food on the thicker pine branches. A beautiful singer, it has a bright yellow throat, black face patch, and black side streaks. Its back and wings are blue-gray and it has two white wing bars.

The little **Brown-headed Nuthatch** (127) probes for food on the pine bark and needle clusters. Its field marks are its brown head, white throat and breast, and white neck spot. Its back is pale blue. Often seen going down tree trunks head-first.

The **Red-cockaded Woodpecker** (128) lives in family groups of up to six. It is identified by its white cheek, black cap, and black-and-white striped back. A very close look will show a tiny spot of red — the cockade — on the upper part of its cheek.

The **Rufous-sided Towhee** (129) is a common bird of the underbrush. It scratches aside leaves searching for food. Identified by its orange-red sides and white outer tail feathers. Males are black on the head, back, and wings. Females are brown where males are black.

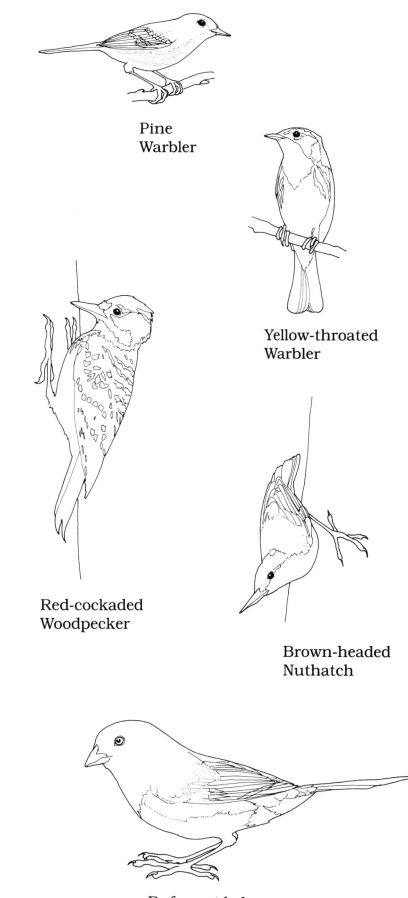

Pine
Warbler

Yellow-throated
Warbler

Red-cockaded
Woodpecker

Brown-headed
Nuthatch

Rufous-sided
Towhee

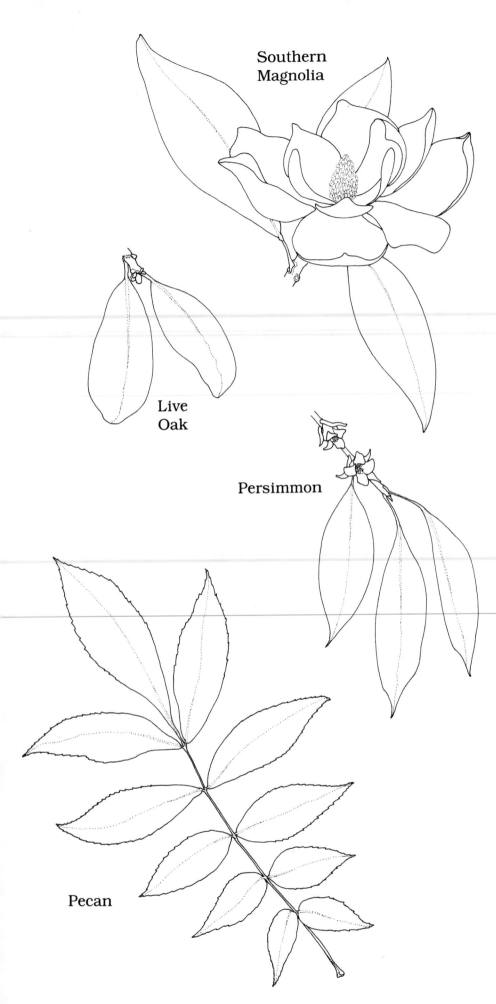

Southern Magnolia

Live Oak

Persimmon

Pecan

Of species of trees associated with the Deep South some are similar to tropical species, while others are related to more northern types.

The **Southern Magnolia** (130) resembles trees of the tropics. It has a simple branching pattern and its dark green leaves are large, thick, waxy, and unlobed, like many trees of the rainforests. The white-petaled flowers are very large and quite fragrant. The stamens and pistils in the center of the flower are yellow.

Live Oak (131) grows in coastal areas. Like the Magnolia, its dark green leaves are evergreen, unlobed and oval, and thick and waxy. It is most notable for its beautiful, widely spreading shape.

Persimmon (132) is, like the Magnolia, a northern member of a tropical family. Its bright green leaves are alternate and rounded, with pointed tips. Small greenish white flowers occur at the bases of the leaves. Mature fruits are orange. Bark is nearly black and resembles alligator hide.

Pecan (133) is a member of the hickory family that produces large tasty nuts. Leaves are compound with up to 17 narrow leaflets. Pecans grow in moist rich soils and can reach heights of over 100 feet.

Baldcypress Swamp Forest

Wet bottomlands of the Southeast are the habitat of **Baldcypress** (134). A majestic tree, growing over 100 feet tall, Baldcypress has delicate yellow-green needles and small rounded cones. The trunk is swollen at the base and the bark is light gray. Underwater roots send up odd, gray, conical knees.

Like most southern trees, Baldcypress is usually laden with wispy clumps of **Spanish Moss** (135), which grow as strands of small gray-green scales with tiny green flowers. Spanish Moss is related to the pineapple, and is not moss at all. It is an "air plant," which grows attached to trees without harming them.

The bright yellow-orange **Prothonotary Warbler** (136) nests in hollow tree cavities. Its tail and wings are blue-gray. It has a vigorous rolling song.

The poisonous **Cottonmouth** or **Water Moccasin** (137) coils at the base of Baldcypresses. It is brown with black bands and a triangular head. Feeds on frogs, fish, and small mammals.

Baldcypress swamps were the habitat of the large **Ivory-billed Woodpecker** (138). This bird had an ivory-colored bill, a tall red crest, and large white wing patches. Its body was black. This bird fed on insects in decaying trees, so it needed fairly large forests with a good number of mature trees. When old forest tracts were cut down, this woodpecker became virtually extinct.

Baldcypress Swamp

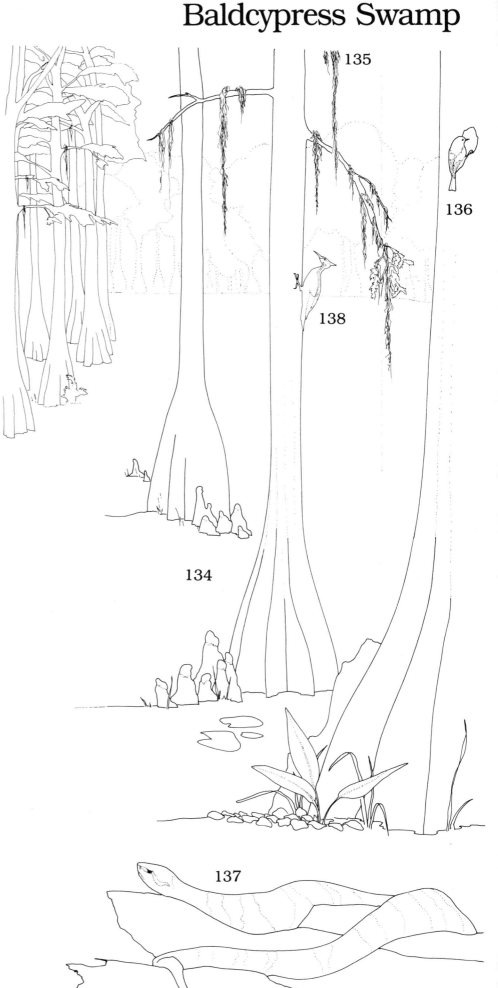

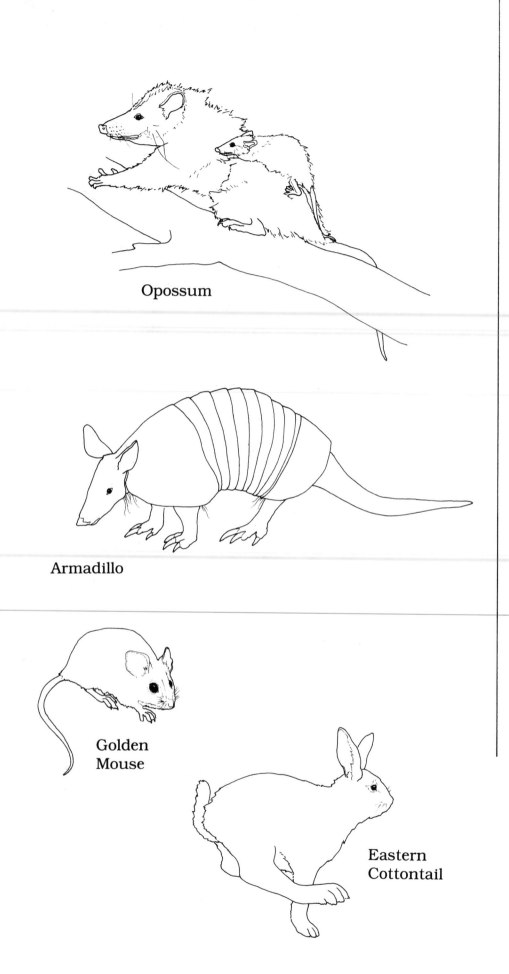

Opossum

Armadillo

Golden
Mouse

Eastern
Cottontail

Southern Mammals

The **Opossum** (139) is abundant throughout the South and is now spreading north. It looks like a large, pale gray rat with a white face, a pinkish naked tail, and pink feet. Its snout is sharply pointed. Opossums are marsupials, and the young develop inside a furry pouch on the mother. The Opossum will commonly hang upside down, using its tail as an extra limb. When in danger it may become limp, seeming to be dead (play possum).

The **Armadillo** (140) resembles an animal in armor. Armadillos are light brown and are covered by bony skin plates. They are usually active at night and burrow during the days. When in danger, they curl into a tight ball.

The tiny **Golden Mouse** (141) inhabits forest thickets and Spanish Moss. Active at night and secretive, but well worth the effort to see it. No other mouse is such a vivid golden color. Undersides are white.

The **Eastern Cottontail** (142) is found in the South, but also lives in all eastern states. Its relatively small ears and white puffy tail are its field marks. The body is grayish brown, and the back of its neck is reddish. The feet are white. The southern Marsh Rabbit (not shown) closely resembles the Cottontail but is darker brown, with chestnut-colored feet.

Southern Hardwoods Birds

The southern hardwoods with their draping of Spanish Moss are the home of several birds uniquely associated with the South.

The Summer Tanager and Northern Cardinal are both red. The **Summer Tanager** (143) is uniformly rose-red with a yellowish bill. The **Northern Cardinal** (144) has a crest and black face with a red bill. Tanagers prefer shade trees, especially oaks, while Cardinals are understory birds, frequenting shrubbery and backyards.

The **Northern Mockingbird** (145) is a slender gray bird with a long tail and white wing patches that show in flight. The Mockingbird is an unequalled mimic and often sings throughout the night.

The multicolored male **Painted Bunting** (146) is an unforgettable sight. He has a bright scarlet throat, breast, and rump, a violet-blue head, and shiny yellow-green back. Painted Buntings are common in shrubs and often sing from telephone wires.

The tiny **Blue-gray Gnatcatcher** (147) resembles a miniature Mockingbird. Its long tail flicks actively as it searches the Spanish Moss for insects. The Gnatcatcher is blue-gray on top, white below. Its tail is black with white outer feathers. Its note is a soft repeated *spee*, with a buzzy quality.

Summer Tanager

Northern Mockingbird

Northern Cardinal

Painted Bunting

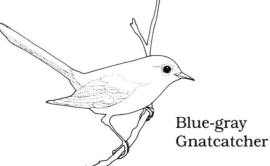

Blue-gray Gnatcatcher

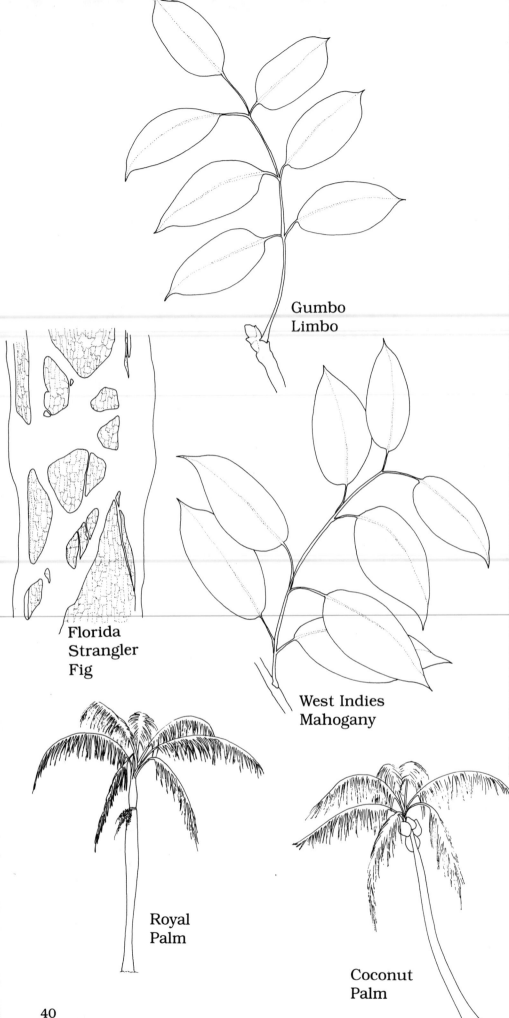

Gumbo
Limbo

Florida
Strangler
Fig

West Indies
Mahogany

Royal
Palm

Coconut
Palm

Subtropical Forest

The southern part of Florida includes a vast freshwater marshland called the Everglades. Within this area are small islands of subtropical forest, where tree branches are covered by air plants, and vines snake down from limbs. Colorful butterflies, birds, tree frogs, and lizards are common.

Gumbo Limbo (148) has very red, smooth bark. Leaves are compound; leaflets are oval, shiny green, and have pointed tips.

Florida Strangler Fig (149) is a woody vine that grows around host trees such as mahogany. The many grayish tendrils of the vine surround the host tree and fuse. As the vine hardens and thickens, it prevents the host tree from growing, thus strangling it. The shiny, dark green leaves are oval with sharply pointed tips.

West Indies Mahogany (150) has leaves similar to those of Gumbo Limbo, but the bark is dark brown and very scaly.

Palms are trees with slender grayish trunks divided by horizontal rings. At the top is a "feather duster" crown of large fanlike leaves.

Royal Palm (151) is straight, growing up to 100 feet tall. The trunk ends in a wide green stem, from which the yellow-green leaves radiate. Clusters of small purple fruits grow from the stem.

Coconut Palm (152) has a gently curved trunk topped by a dense cluster of large yellow-green leaves, under which grow the coconuts. Coconuts begin green, then ripen into large brown husks.

Life in Subtropical Trees

Living atop the limbs of Gumbo Limbo and Bald-cypress are a variety of air plants and animals. Like Spanish Moss, the air plants are not parasites, and do no harm to their host trees.

Tillandsia (153) is sometimes called Wild Pine, but it is not a pine at all. It is a bromeliad, and is a close relative of pineapple and Spanish Moss. Its bright red spikes are not flowers but bracts. The inconspicuous flowers are enclosed by the bracts. Stiff gray-green leaves that surround the flower stalk trap rainwater. The plant gets vital minerals from the water.

Butterfly Orchid (154) is recognized by the wide fleshy swellings at its base, called pseudobulbs. These structures store water that the orchid uses during the dry season. Two long green leaves arise from each pseudobulb. Flowers are small, with many on a single stalk. Each fragrant flower has a deep red center and a large white lip. Yellow-green petals surround the lip petal.

The **Zebra Butterfly** (155) is instantly recognized by its slender shape and bold black wings with bright yellow bars. A member of a tropical group, the Zebra is a slow weak flier. Its bright coloration is thought to be a warning to predators that it is very distasteful.

Liguus Tree Snails (156) are as diversely colored as the rainbow. Some have light blue bands with narrow gold bands inside. Some have reddish bands alternating with blue, white, and brown. All are beautiful. Tree Snails feed on tiny plants living on tree bark. During heavy rains they move to the ground to mate.

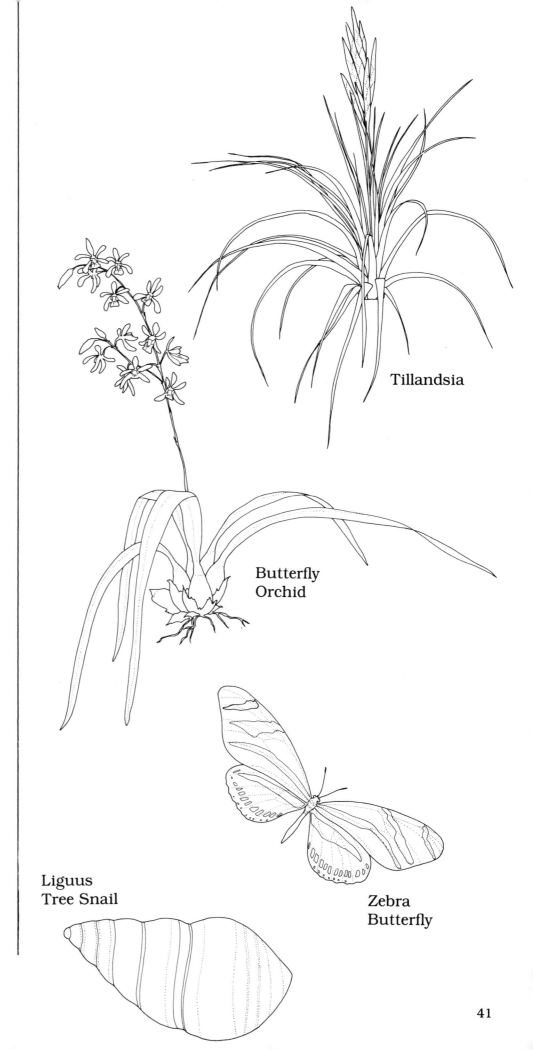

Tillandsia

Butterfly Orchid

Liguus Tree Snail

Zebra Butterfly

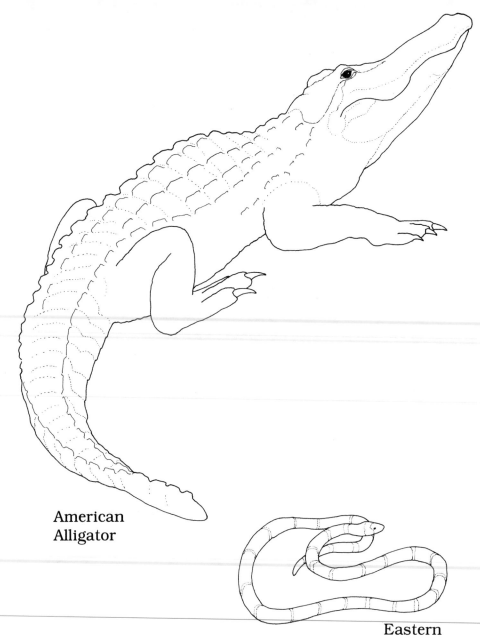

American
Alligator

Subtropical Reptiles and Amphibians

The **American Alligator** (157), a superb swimmer, grows up to 15 feet long, and has a flattened tail, large head with a blunt snout, and raised eyes. It is mostly black with yellowish brown bands that are faint in adults but bright in juveniles. Feeds on fish, frogs, birds, and mammals.

The **Eastern Coral Snake** (158) is colorful but deadly. *It should not be handled.* On the Coral Snake the red bands touch the yellow bands — "red and yellow, kill a fellow." But on the similar but non-poisonous King Snake red touches black — "red and black, friend of Jack."

The **Green Anole** (159) is a small lizard that can change its body color from brown to green. It has a very pointed snout and a loose flap of pink skin hanging from its throat. Usually seen scurrying along the ground or climbing up a palm trunk.

The **Cuban Treefrog** (160) is large, up to 6 inches long, with prominent toe pads. Color can vary from light green to brown. Its voice is a deep snore.

Eastern
Coral Snake

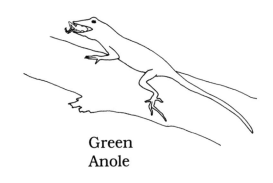

Green
Anole

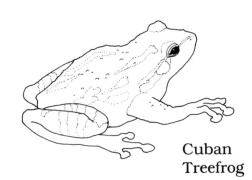

Cuban
Treefrog

Birds of Prey

The subtropical forest and surrounding Everglades are home to several interesting birds of prey.

The **Swallow-tailed Kite** (161) is an active flier, slicing through the air in pursuit of large insects. Its deeply forked, all-black tail is distinctive. Its head and undersides are all white and its back is black.

The **Snail Kite** (162) is very stocky with a red, hooked bill and white rump. Males are blue-gray, females are brown with streaked breasts. Formerly called the Everglade Kite, the Snail Kite feeds only on one kind of large snail.

The **Red-shouldered Hawk** (163) is found throughout the eastern U.S., but is very abundant in southern Florida. Its tail is heavily barred with black and white and each shoulder has a reddish brown patch. The body is barred with brown. This hawk frequently perches on telephone poles.

The **Bald Eagle** (164) is very large with a white head and tail. The body is brown. Bald eagles are rare in most parts of the U.S., but are common in southern Florida and Alaska.

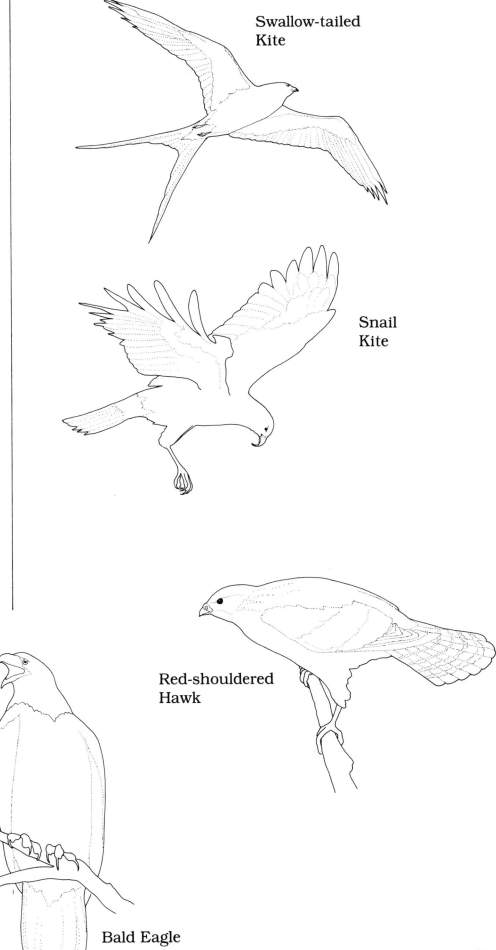

Swallow-tailed Kite

Snail Kite

Red-shouldered Hawk

Bald Eagle

White-crowned
Pigeon

American
Crocodile

Mangrove Forest

The south Florida Coast and Keys are covered by mangrove forest. Mangroves are short dense trees that tolerate salt water.

The **Red Mangrove** (165) is named for its reddish bark. Its numerous aerial or prop roots help anchor it in soft mud. The prop roots also provide places where oysters and other marine animals can grow. The floating, podlike mangrove seedlings can survive well in salt water. Leaves are thick, leathery, and dark green.

The **Manatee** (166) swims in the channels that weave through the mangroves. Manatees are large gray mammals with wide, doglike heads and flat, paddle-shaped tails. The forelegs are flippers.

The **American Crocodile** (167) is a rare inhabitant of mangrove areas. Its light brown color and sharply pointed snout distinguish it from the American Alligator (p. 42).

Many birds roost and nest in the mangroves. The Wood Stork and White Ibis both have downcurving bills. The **Wood Stork** (168) is larger with a grayish face and neck and black legs. In flight, its underwings show extensive black. The **White Ibis** (169) has a red bill and face and red legs. In flight, only its wing tips are black.

The Roseate Spoonbill and American Flamingo are both reddish-pink. The **Roseate Spoonbill**'s (170) wide, greenish bill is flattened at the tip. It has pink on its wings and deep red shoulders, but its neck and back are white. The tail is or-angy and the head is grayish green. This bird probes mud for worms and other animals. **American Flamingos** (171) are uniformly pink with long legs and necks. Wings show black linings in flight. The bill has a strong downward bend and functions to strain tiny animals from the water.

The **Brown Pelican** (172) has a huge bill with an expandable pouch. Its body is gray-brown with a chestnut neck and yellow face bordered by white. Dives from the air for fish.

The **White-crowned Pigeon** (173) looks like a domestic pigeon in shape and size, but is uniformly dark blue with a white-cap. It nests in the mangroves and is found only in the Florida Keys.

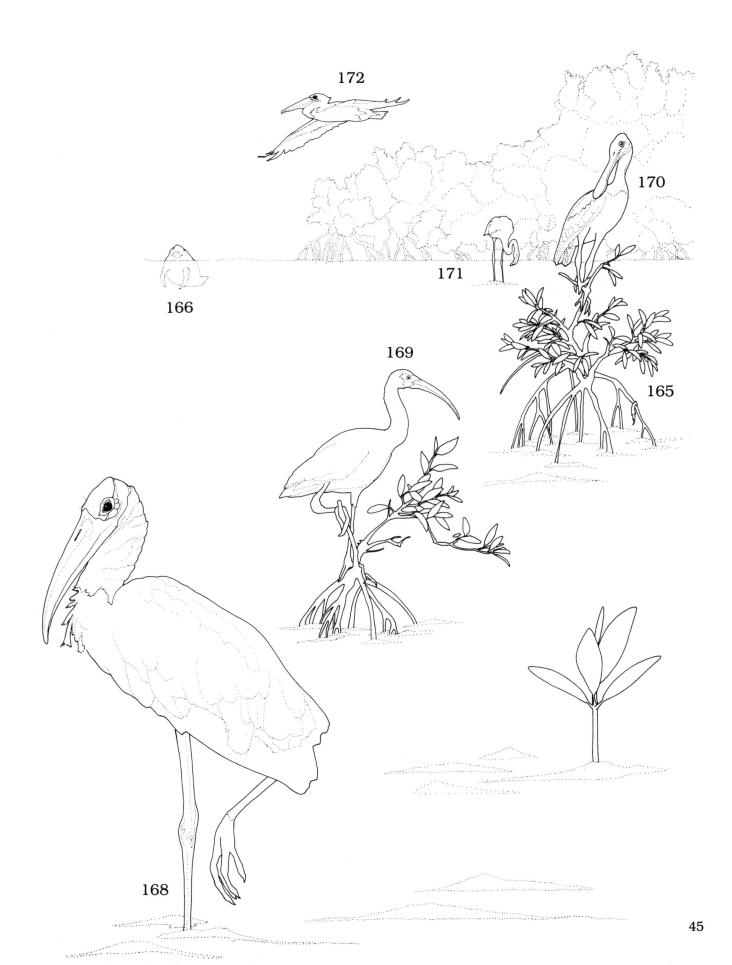

172

170

171

166

169

165

168

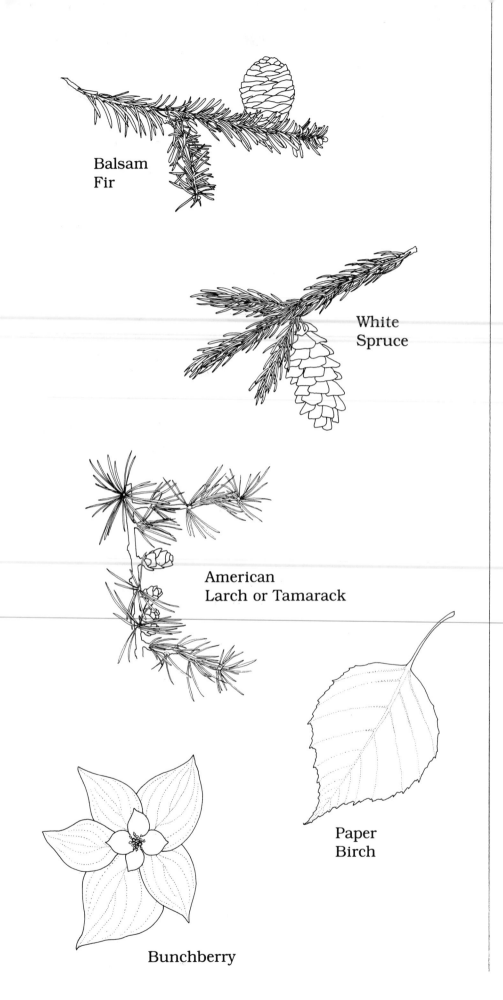

Balsam
Fir

White
Spruce

American
Larch or Tamarack

Paper
Birch

Bunchberry

Boreal Forest

The boreal forest covers most of the northern United States and Canada. It is a dense forest of evergreen conifers, such as the spruces and firs commonly selected as Christmas trees. The forest floor is soft from the accumulation of fallen needles.

Firs and spruces are cone-shaped trees with dense short needles. Spruce needles feel prickly; those of firs are softer. Cones hang downward from spruce branches; on firs the cones are upright.

Balsam Fir (174) has flattened, short, dark green needles that tend to curve upward. Cones are bluish gray with compact closed scales.

White Spruce (175) has square-shaped, dark green needles that leave tiny pegs on the branch when they fall off. Needles curve toward the tip of the branch. Cones are brownish and long with open scales.

The **American Larch** or **Tamarack** (176) is an unusual conifer because it drops its needles in winter. Needles are soft, blue-green, and triangular in cross section. They grow in small bundles along the length of the branch. Tamarack needles are not as dense as those of spruces or firs, giving the tree a feathery appearance. Before dropping in the fall, the needles turn yellow.

Paper Birch (177) is recognized by its bright white, peeling bark, once used for canoes. Leaves are light green, heart-shaped, toothed, and sharply pointed.

Bunchberry (178) is a boreal wildflower. Tiny yellow-green flowers are surrounded by four large, white, petal-like bracts and a whorl of oval leaves. Produces big, bright red berries.

Animals of the Boreal Forest

The chunky **Spruce Grouse** (179) walks like a chicken. The male is blue-gray on the back and wings; its rounded black tail has a light brown band at the tip. A tiny spot of red skin can be seen above each eye. Females are brown with heavy barring. Often very tame and easy to approach.

The **Gray Jay** (180) is large, dark gray on the back, wings, and tail, with a black patch on the back of its head. Its face, throat, and breast are grayish white. The Gray Jay is also called a "Whiskey Jack" and often becomes tame at campgrounds.

The **Moose** (181) is the largest hoofed mammal in the U.S. It is uniformly blackish brown with long legs and a long drooping face. Males have a wide rack of broad, flat antlers and a black "beard" that hangs from their throats. The boreal forest is also called the "spruce-moose forest."

The **Wolverine** (182) is a large member of the weasel family. It is stocky with a thick, furred tail, and resembles a small bear. It is dark brown with wide, buffy side stripes that meet at the tail base. It also has a buffy streak across the head behind its eyes. The Wolverine is known for its fearlessness in attacking larger animals.

The **Red Squirrel** (183) is quite rufous, especially on its bushy tail. Underparts are white; the eyes are surrounded by a large white eye-ring. Red squirrels frequently scold observers, vigorously thrashing their tails as they call.

Spruce Grouse

Gray Jay

Moose

Wolverine

Red Squirrel

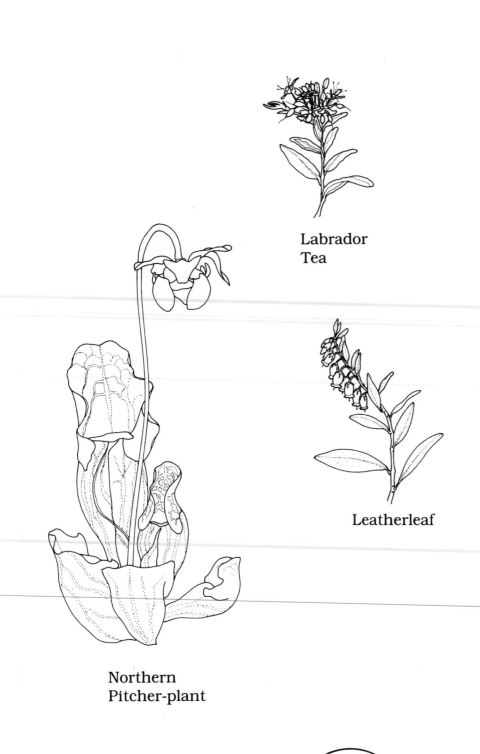

Labrador
Tea

Leatherleaf

Northern
Pitcher-plant

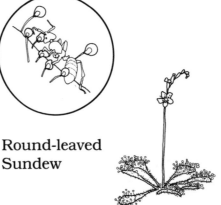

Round-leaved
Sundew

Bogs

Scattered within the boreal forest are shrubby areas of very soft ground, often so soft that it moves or quakes as you walk over it. These areas are bogs, which are actually lakes and ponds that have slowly filled. There is often open water in the center of bogs. Bogs are also found throughout the Northeast. Where they occur, the boreal-forest species extend their range far south of the northern boreal forest.

Labrador Tea and Leatherleaf are common bog shrubs. **Laborador Tea** (184) is evergreen, with alternate, elongate, oval leaves. Leaves feel very leathery; they are green above but orange and fuzzy below. Clusters of small white flowers grow from the branch tips. **Leatherleaf** (185) leaves are similar, but with tiny teeth along the margins. Flowers are white but not clustered. They are bell-shaped and hang in a row beneath the branch.

Insectivorous plants, which trap and digest insects, are common in bogs. The **Northern Pitcher-plant** (186) has large funnel-shaped leaves with wide lips. Leaves have hairs that point inward, trapping insects that have entered. Flowers are large and deep red.

Round-leaved **Sundew** (187) has leaves covered with moist sticky hairs that trap insects. Flowers are small and white.

Animals of the Bogs

Many birds nest in and around bogs. The grayish brown **Olive-sided Flycatcher** (188) sits out in the open. Field marks are its upright posture, dark brown, triangular head, wing bars, and white tufts between its wings and back. Its call is a sharp *Hip, three cheers!*

The **Cedar Waxwing** (189) also sits upright but has a crest and a yellow band across the tip of its tail. Warm brown with a black face and throat, the waxwing has tiny, red, waxlike tips on some of its wing feathers. It feeds heavily on fruit.

The **Nashville Warbler** (190) inhabits dense shrubs. It has a combination of a gray head, white eye-ring and yellow throat. Its back and wings are olive-green.

In bogs in Connecticut, New York, and New Jersey lives the **Bog Turtle** (191). It is identified by the large orange spot behind its eyes and faint orange markings on its brown shell.

The **Bog Lemming** (192) is a small mouse with a short tail and tiny ears. It is uniform grayish brown. Its runways can often be seen among the bog grasses.

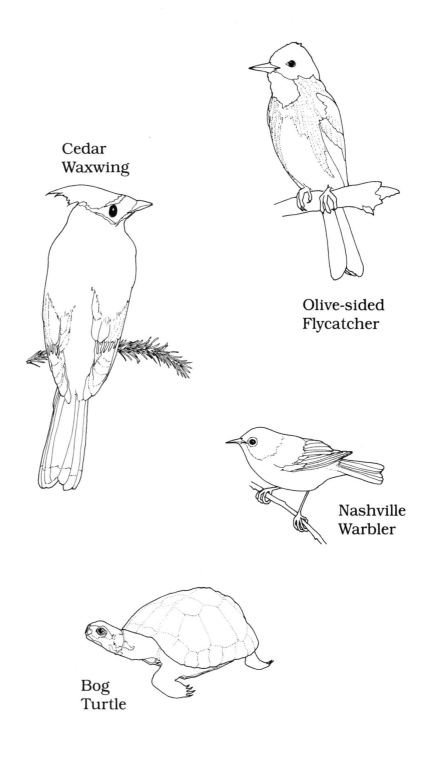

Cedar Waxwing

Olive-sided Flycatcher

Nashville Warbler

Bog Turtle

Bog Lemming

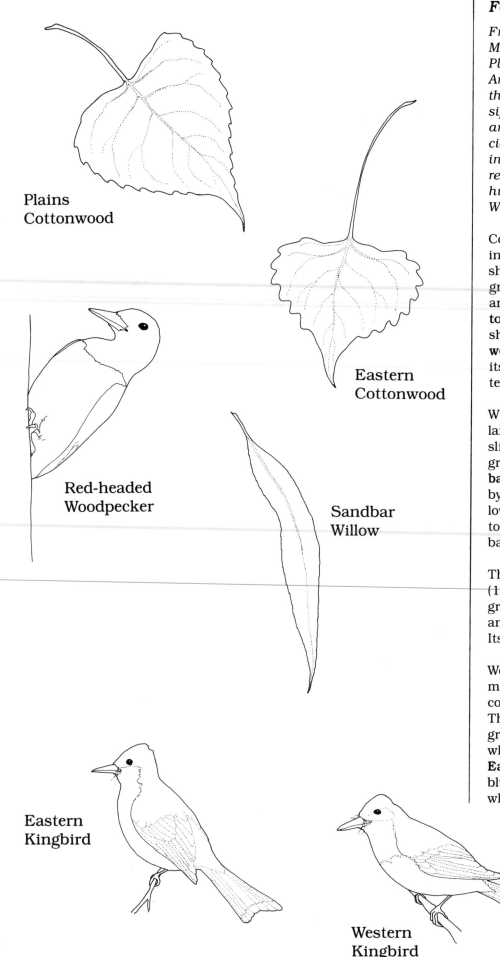

Plains
Cottonwood

Eastern
Cottonwood

Red-headed
Woodpecker

Sandbar
Willow

Eastern
Kingbird

Western
Kingbird

Riverine Cottonwood Forest

From their origins in the Rocky Mountains, rivers such as the Platte, the Missouri, and the Arkansas flow eastward across the Great Plains to the Mississippi. Although the plains are arid, the rivers provide sufficient moisture to the surrounding soil to support trees. The result is a ribbon of forest that hugs the rivers across the West.

Cottonwoods are wide spreading trees that provide much shade. Leaves are bright yellow-green, alternate, triangular, and long-stalked. **Eastern Cottonwood** (194) leaves are sharply toothed. **Plains Cottonwood** (193) is very similar but its leaves have blunt rounded teeth.

Willows have alternate, slender, lancelike leaves that are usually slightly toothed. They often grow densely like shrubs. **Sandbar Willow** (195) is identified by its very slender, toothed, yellowish green leaves. It is quick to colonize newly created sandbars along the rivers.

The **Red-headed Woodpecker** (196) is common in cottonwood groves. It has an all-red head and large white wing patches. Its back and tail are blue-black.

Western and Eastern Kingbirds may feed together in the same cottonwood as East meets West. The **Western Kingbird** (197) is gray with a yellow breast and white outer tail feathers. The **Eastern Kingbird** (198) is dark blue with a white breast and white tail band.

Arizona Sycamore Canyon Forest

Scattered throughout southern Arizona are tall rocky canyons with streams running through them. These canyons provide a green oasis in what is otherwise a desert.

The **Arizona Sycamore** (199) is abundant in the canyons. It has whitish brown bark that peels off in patches. The alternate leaves have five (sometimes seven) deep lobes.

The **Elegant Trogon** (200), one of the most glamorous birds in the U.S., nests in sycamore cavities. Males have bright red breasts, white breast bands, and shiny, dark green heads and backs. The upper surface of the long square tail is rusty, the undersurface pale gray with thin black bars. Most Trogons are native to the tropics, and only the Elegant Trogon nests in North America.

The Sulfur-bellied Flycatcher and Bridled Titmouse also nest in sycamore cavities. Like the Trogon, the **Sulfur-bellied Flycatcher** (201) is from the tropics. Its black-streaked yellow breast, dark eye line, and rufous tail identify it. Its back and wings are light brown with black streaks. The **Bridled Titmouse** (202) is crested, uniformly gray, with a bold black eye line and cheek stripe.

Small bands of **Collared Peccaries** (203) or Javelinas feed in sycamore canyons. Identified by its piglike body and white shoulder stripe, the peccary is black with a pink nose at the tip of its snout.

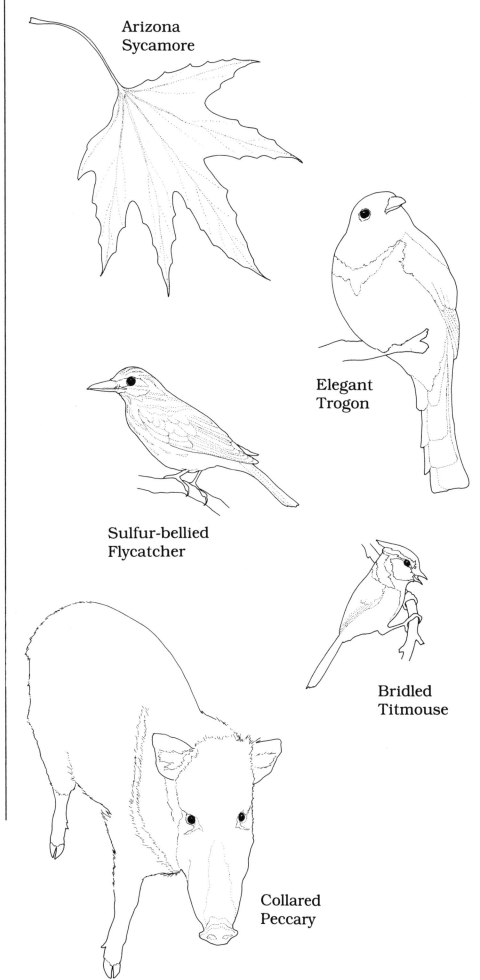

Arizona Sycamore

Elegant Trogon

Sulfur-bellied Flycatcher

Bridled Titmouse

Collared Peccary

Pinyon-Juniper Forest

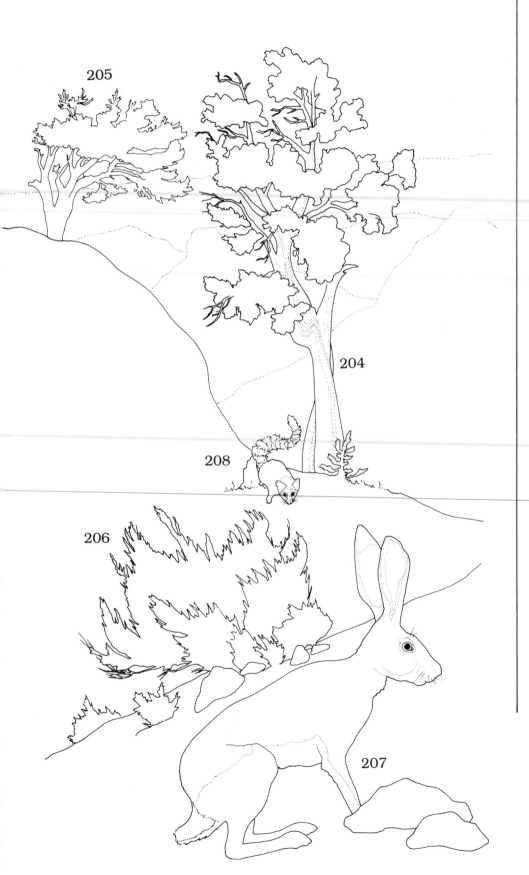

205

204

208

206

207

In semi-arid land from the foothills of the Rockies throughout the southwestern states is an open forest of bushy trees. Rarely taller than 30 feet, this pygmy forest is composed of several species of Pinyon Pines and western Junipers.

Pinyon Pines (204) have short needles (1–1½ inches) and small cones. Needles are yellow-green, in bundles of two. Cones contain large seeds, which are eaten by many animals, as well as by people.

Junipers (205) are short shrubby trees, with several trunks often coming from a single base. Rather than nee-dles, Junipers have tiny, over-lapping, yellow-green scales. Cones resemble berries and are brown.

Sagebrush (206) is an abun-dant shrub. Its leaves are pale grayish green and terminate in three small lobes. The leaves are very pungent, the odor of sage.

The **Blacktail Jackrabbit** (207) has very long, black-tipped ears. Its body is buffy-gray, and its short tail is black on top and white below. Its rump is blackish brown.

The **Ringtail** (208) or Cacomis-tle is a distant relative of the raccoon that hunts mice and ground squirrels. Its body is yellowish gray, with a bushy, black-and-white ringed tail. It has a pointed snout, and its dark eyes are circled by wide white eye-rings. There is a black spot between the eyes.

The **Pinyon Jay** (209) forages for food in flocks. Its field marks are its short tail and stocky build, long beak, and solid, deep blue color. Local numbers of jays increase when pinyon nuts (seeds) are abundant.

The **Black-billed Magpie** (210) often feeds on road kills (animals that have been hit by cars). It is easy to identify. No other large bird is bold black and white with a long, shiny green tail.

The **Black-throated Gray Warbler** (211) is common in pygmy forests. Its name describes it well. It has a black throat, black cap, and wide black line through its eyes. Its back is grayish blue, and its breast is white. Very close views reveal a tiny spot of yellow in front of each eye.

The **Collared Lizard** (212) has a long green tail spotted with black. Its back is green with yellow spots and streaks, and its head is brownish green. The upper surface of its neck has two wide, black rings separated by buff. Collared lizards can stand up and run swiftly on their long hind legs.

The **Tarantula** (213) is a large spider that is mostly active at night. Its hairy body and large size are unmistakable. Its legs are black but its body is a warm brown. Its bite can be painful but does not usually cause serious harm to humans.

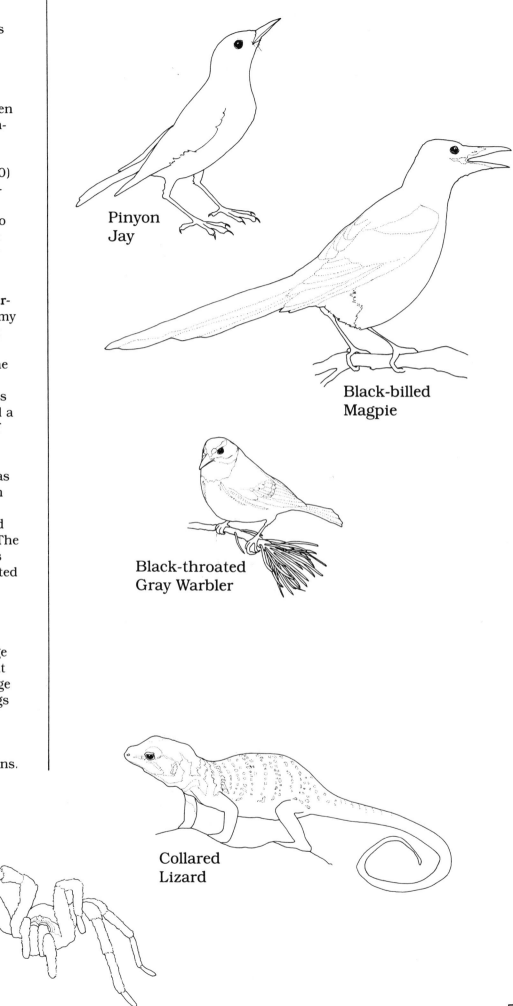

Pinyon Jay

Black-billed Magpie

Black-throated Gray Warbler

Collared Lizard

Tarantula

Ponderosa Pine Forest

216

214

217

215

218

Ponderosa Pine Forest

Midway in elevation between the high mountains and flat deserts of the West are open, parklike forests of Ponderosa Pines. Often called a transition zone, Ponderosa Pine forests are in-between cool mountain spruce-fir forests and arid pinyon-juniper forests.

Ponderosa Pine (214) grows straight and tall, up to 180 feet. The bark is reddish orange, grows in small scaly plates, and emits a faint odor that resembles the smell of vanilla extract. Needles are 10 inches long, in bundles of two or three. Prickly cones are 6 inches long.

The **Stellar's Jay** (215) frequents campsites and picnic areas. Identified by its tall black crest and blue body, the "western blue jay" feeds on pine nuts and picnic scraps.

The **Western Bluebird** (216) has a dark blue throat and head with reddish breast, sides, and back. It prefers grassy openings in the forest where it catches insects on the wing.

The **Tassle-eared Squirrel** (217) has long reddish ear tufts and a bushy white tail. Its body is grayish and its back is reddish.

The **Golden-mantled Ground Squirrel** (218) looks like a large chipmunk. It has a bright orange face and white side stripes. Its underbelly is white and it has a white eye-ring. Its back is gray-brown.

Ponderosa Pine Forest Birds

The Ponderosa Pine forests are the habitat of many birds, including several that are more common in Mexico. The following species often feed together in flocks.

The **Mexican Chickadee** (219) is recognized by its large black bib, which extends to its breast, It has a black cap, white face, and gray body. It is found only in the mountains of Arizona, New Mexico, and Texas.

The **Pygmy Nuthatch** (220) is very small, with a blue-gray back, an olive-green head, and a white throat and breast. It has a thin black line through each eye. As they search for food, Pygmys utter a constant, high, *pip pip* note.

The **Red-faced Warbler** (221) has a brilliant scarlet face and throat, plus a black cap extending below its eyes. Its body is otherwise gray.

The **Painted Redstart** (222) is unmistakable. Its black body, white outer tail feathers, white wing patch, and red underbelly are a combination found in no other species. It flits butterfly-like from tree to tree with its tail and wings partially spread, as it catches flying insects close to the ground.

The **Olive Warbler** (223) is identified by its two distinct wing bars and gray color. The male has a warm orange-buff head with a black eye-mask. Searches for insects high in the pines.

Mexican Chickadee

Pygmy Nuthatch

Red-faced Warbler

Painted Redstart

Olive Warbler

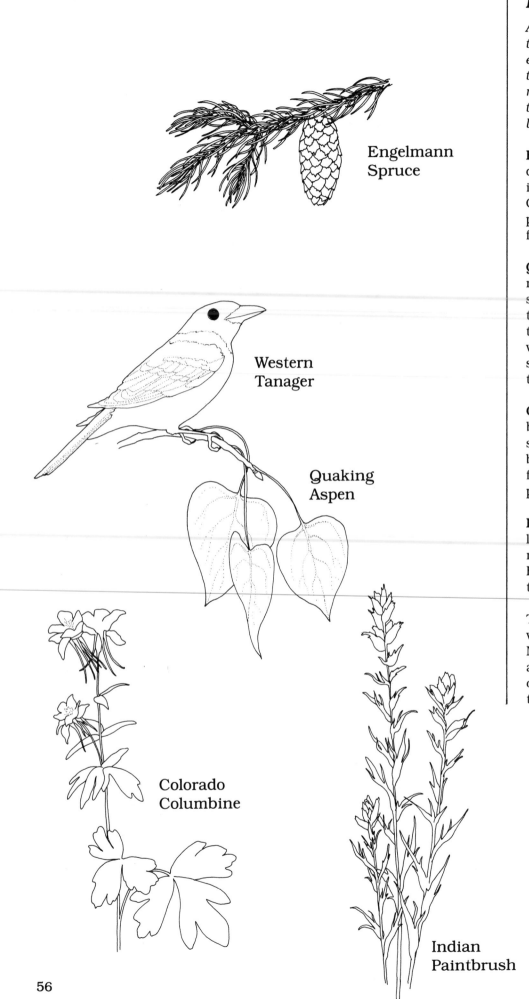

Engelmann
Spruce

Western
Tanager

Quaking
Aspen

Colorado
Columbine

Indian
Paintbrush

Rocky Mountain Forest

At high elevations throughout the Rocky Mountains are forests of spruce and fir. After disturbances such as fires, these needle-bearing trees may be temporarily replaced by broad-leaved Quaking Aspens.

Engelmann Spruce (224) needles are soft, 1¼ inches or less in length, and dark blue-green. Cones are covered with papery pointed scales. May grow to 80 feet.

Quaking Aspen (225) is so named because its wide, heart-shaped leaves tremble in even the mildest breeze. Leaves are toothed, pale green above, and white on the underside. Bark is smooth and yellowish. Aspens turn brilliant gold in autumn.

Colorado Columbine (226) is a bright white, five-petaled flower surrounded by long violet bracts. At night sphinx moths feed on the nectar and spread pollen.

Indian Paintbrush (227) has long tubular flowers surrounded by bright red bracts. Hummingbirds are attracted by the red color.

The **Western Tanager** (228) is very common in aspen groves. Males are yellow and black with a red face. Females are yellow-olive and are best identified by their two wing bars.

Rocky Mountain Animals

Mountain meadows and forests are the summer habitat of **Elk** (229) or Wapiti. Male Elk are distinguished from deer by their greater size; large rack of antlers; dark brown, shaggy necks; and pale yellowish rump. Their body is warm brown. Females lack antlers and are less shaggy on the neck. Elk migrate down the mountains to winter in the valleys.

Bighorn Sheep (230) prefer high rocky areas near the limit of tree growth. Only males have the large coiled horns. Both sexes are buffy-brown with bright white rumps. Bighorn males (rams) are noted for their remarkable contests of head clashing.

The **Yellowbelly Marmot** (231) prefers the rocky slopes above tree line. Resembling a large woodchuck, the Marmot is yellowish brown with a white mark across its face. Lives in underground dens, often sitting upright at the entrance. Makes a loud shrill whistle.

The gray and black **Clark's Nutcracker** (232) is common throughout the Rockies. In flight it shows white wing patches and white outer tail feathers. Noisy and conspicuous, the Nutcracker often swoops into campsites in search of food.

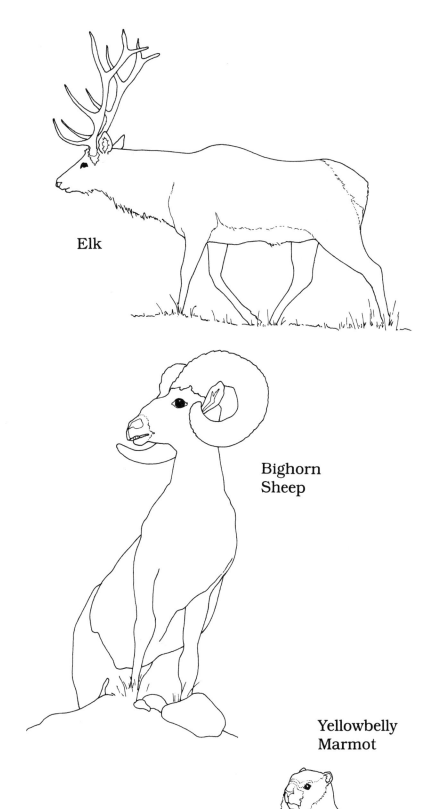

Elk

Bighorn Sheep

Yellowbelly Marmot

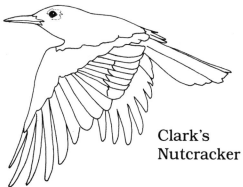

Clark's Nutcracker

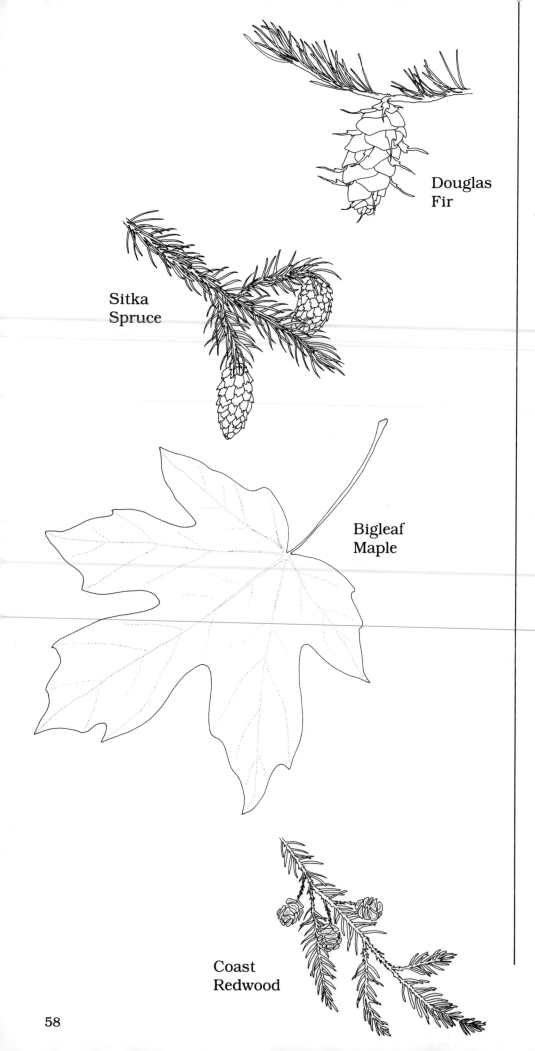

Douglas
Fir

Sitka
Spruce

Bigleaf
Maple

Coast
Redwood

Pacific Coast Forest

The Pacific Coast, from northern California to Alaska, is a land of giant trees. The cool Pacific Ocean waters reduce air temperature to bathe coastal forests in a constant mist. This climate provides superb growing conditions, which result in coastal rain forests.

The **Douglas Fir** (233) often exceeds 250 feet. On mature trees the dark brown trunk may rise 100 feet before any horizontal branches appear. The diameter of the trunk is 4-6 feet. Branches appear to droop, and are covered by small, 1½-inch light green needles. Cones are only 3-4 inches long with distinctive three-pointed bracts protruding from between the scales.

Sitka Spruce (234) can exceed 200 feet in height with a trunk diameter of 6 feet. Yellow-green needles are about ½ inch long, stiff, and very prickly. Cones are orange-brown and appear ragged and scaly, often growing in clusters at the branch tips. Bark is quite reddish.

Bigleaf Maple (235) is common in the groves of giant conifers. Looking like a huge Sugar Maple, the Bigleaf can exceed 100 feet in height. Its leaves, which turn golden-brown in fall, each with five deep lobes, are about 1 foot wide! No other maple has such huge leaves.

Coast Redwood (236) is very tall and slender. It commonly reaches 250 feet, but can top 350 feet. Redwoods thrive in groves along the fogbound coast of northern California. Branches hang loosely with soft, delicate yellow-green needles. Cones are tiny, about 1 inch long. The tree is named for its very reddish bark and wood.

Pacific Forest Birds

The tall, deeply shaded conifer forests provide a habitat for a variety of birds.

High among the needle-laden branches, the **Townsend's Warbler** (237) gleans insects. The male has a bold face pattern of yellow and black, a yellow breast, and black streaks along its sides. The insectlike wheezy song is heard more often than the bird is seen.

Flocks of **Chestnut-backed Chickadees** (238) forage among conifers. Easily recognized by its rusty back and sooty cap, the Chestnut-back often flocks with other bird species, such as warblers. Its call is a sharp *zee zee.*

Foraging along the forest floor is the robinlike **Varied Thrush** (239). It has an orange breast and orange wing bars, a black breast band, and black cheeks. Its back is steel blue, but looks black in dim forest light.

The western race of the **Dark-eyed Junco** (240) is called the Oregon Junco. It has a dark gray hood, reddish brown back, and pale rusty sides. As it flies up from the forest floor, it shows its white outer tail feathers.

The **Blue Grouse** (241) is the chicken of the forest. Males are dusky blue-gray with a black tail ending in a gray band. A patch of yellow skin above each eye is visible at close range. When courting, males reveal yellow air sacs on their breasts. When inflated, these sacs help make a robust hooting call.

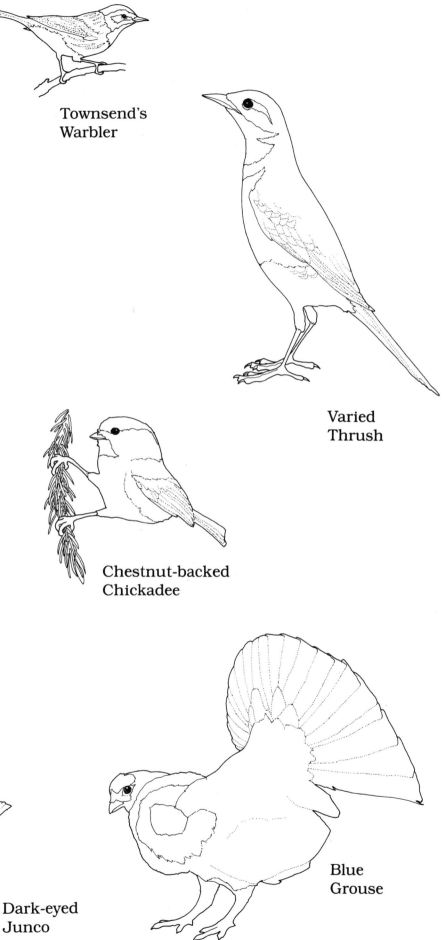

Townsend's
Warbler

Varied
Thrush

Chestnut-backed
Chickadee

Dark-eyed
Junco

Blue
Grouse

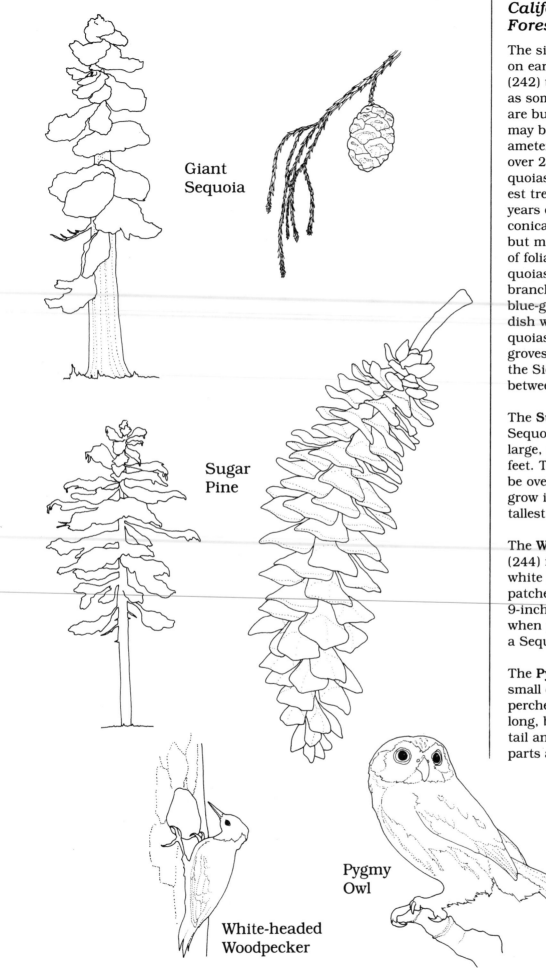

Giant
Sequoia

Sugar
Pine

White-headed
Woodpecker

Pygmy
Owl

California Sequoia Forest

The single largest living things on earth are **Giant Sequoia** (242) trees. Though not as tall as some Redwoods, Sequoias are bulky: a 250-foot-tall tree may be more than 30 feet in diameter at the base and weigh over 2 million pounds! Sequoias are also among the oldest trees, some being over 3000 years old. Young Sequoias are conical like Christmas trees, but mature trees have patches of foliage in dense clusters. Sequoias lack needles but have branches covered with prickly blue-green scales. Bark is reddish with deep furrows. Sequoias grow in 75 scattered groves on the western side of the Sierra Nevada, at elevations between 5000 and 7000 feet.

The **Sugar Pine** (243) shares Sequoia groves and is also large, growing to heights of 200 feet. The light brown cones can be over 2 feet in length! Needles grow in bundles of five on this tallest of American pines.

The **White-headed Woodpecker** (244) is easily identified by its white head, white wing patches, and black body. This 9-inch bird can look very tiny when probing the bark high in a Sequoia.

The **Pygmy Owl** (245) is a very small owl often seen in daytime perched on an exposed limb. Its long, black-and-white, barred tail and streaked brown underparts are reliable field marks.

Western Alpine Forest

High in the mountains of Nevada and California grow the world's oldest organisms. Some **Bristlecone Pines** (246) have lived for over 4000 years! Because of the harsh mountaintop climate, Bristlecones grow so slowly that ancient individuals may be only 30 feet tall. Cones have sharp curving prickles. Blue-green needles with white resin spots grow in bundles of five.

The **Whitebark Pine** (247) is common at high elevations throughout the West. It also has needles in bundles of five, but has rounded cones that are not prickly. Bark is pale grayish. Like many high altitude trees, Whitebark Pines often assume a shrublike growth form. This is because tall limbs are killed by the freezing winter winds, but branches that grow outward at ground level are protected by the blanket of winter snow.

Rocky outcrops are the habitat of **Western Juniper** (248), identified by its green scaly foliage; tiny, blue, fleshy cones; and gnarled cinnamon-colored bark.

Among the boulders are the burrows of the small gray-brown **Pika** (249). Pikas spend the summer gathering plant material, which they store in their burrows and feed on in winter. Pikas are related to rabbits, but are more vocal, emitting a high-pitched bleat, like a tiny goat.

The **Gray-crowned Rosy Finch** (250) nests in cavities among the rocks. The rosy rump and wing patch and gray head identify this most alpine of birds. The body is deep reddish brown.

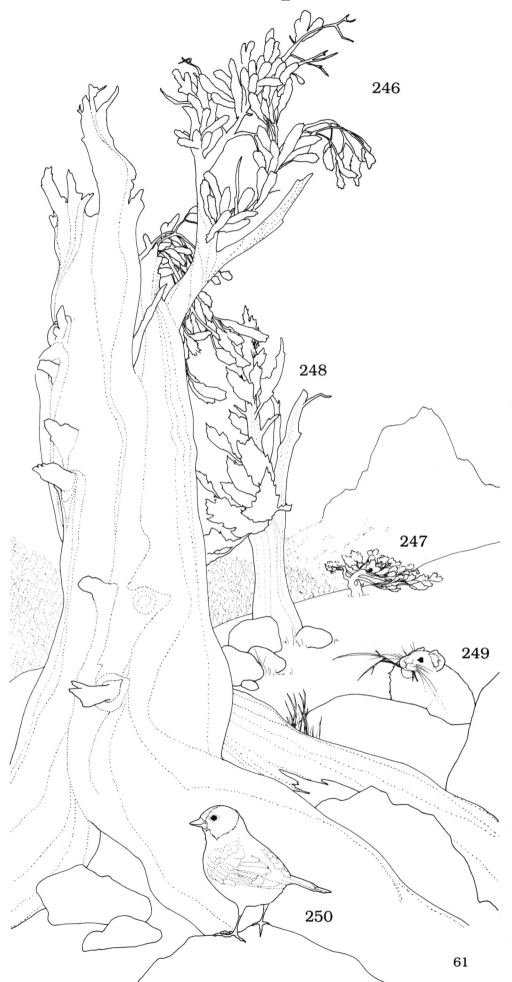

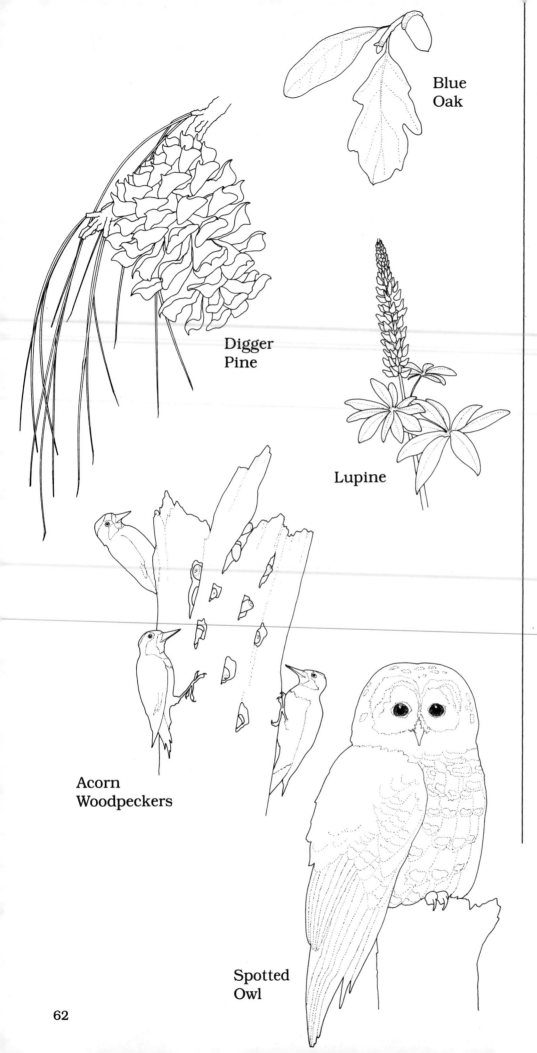

Blue Oak

Digger Pine

Lupine

Acorn Woodpeckers

Spotted Owl

Western Oak Forest

Along the foothills of the Sierra Nevada is an open, parklike forest of scattered small trees, consisting mostly of Blue Oak and Digger Pine. Neither tree normally grows taller than 60 feet.

Blue Oak (251) has small, bluish, leathery leaves of various shapes — unlobed, partially lobed, or deeply lobed. Bark is scaly and grayish. The acorn is elongated with a small cup.

Digger Pine (252) is most easily recognized by its grayish green needles. The stiff needles are 7–13 inches long, and grow in bundles of three. Cones are 6–10 inches long, oval, with open scales curving toward the branch.

Lupines (253) are common from foothills to mountain meadows. They have long, upright spikes of blue-violet flowers. Some may grow five feet tall. Leaves radiate like spokes from the central stem.

Groups of **Acorn Woodpeckers** (254) store caches of acorns in tree trunks and telephone poles. This conspicuous bird is identified by its black back; white wing patches and rump; and bold black, white, and red face pattern.

The **Spotted Owl** (255) spends its days roosting within the dense foliage along canyon streams. At night it hunts rodents. Field marks are its brown eyes; rounded head without ear tufts; and dark brown, heavily-barred feathers.

Chaparral

On hot dry slopes of the Southern California foothills grows a shrub forest so dense that it is impenetrable in places. This odd forest is called by the Spanish name, chaparral. *In spite of recurring lightning-started fires, the plants of this forest are able to resprout quickly because of their fire-resistant seeds.*

The **Whiteleaf Manzanita** (256) is very common. It has distinctive reddish bark, crooked stems, and dull green, leathery, oval leaves. Drooping clusters of bell-shaped flowers are colored white to rose.

Common Buckbrush (257) is recognized in spring by its clusters of small, white, fragrant flowers. Leaves are opposite; narrow at the base; wide and rounded at the tip.

The **Scrub Jay** (258) is common in oak woodlands and chaparral. It has no crest. This jay is blue with a grayish throat, black cheek patch, and rusty back. It is often found in small but noisy flocks.

The **Wrentit** (259) is found only in chaparral. Though noisy, this slender, brown, chickadee-sized bird is hard to glimpse in the dense shrubs. Its bright yellow eye and long tail are good field marks.

The **California Quail** (260) is often seen along roadsides. Its chickenlike shape, black topknot, black face and throat, and scaly gray breast make it easy to recognize.

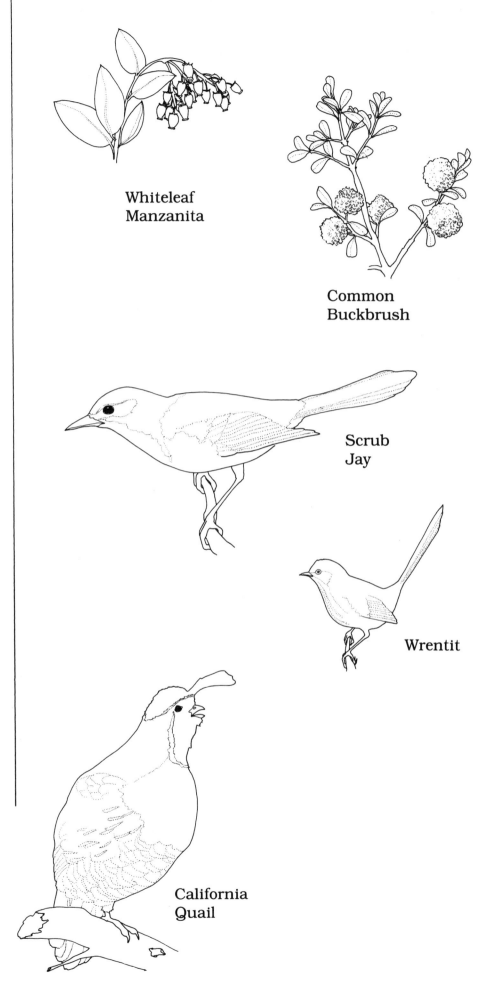

Whiteleaf
Manzanita

Common
Buckbrush

Scrub
Jay

Wrentit

California
Quail

Extinct and Threatened Species

Although our country is scarcely over 200 years old, the United States has already suffered the loss of several species. During this century, a conservation ethic has established itself; endangered and threatened species are now protected by law.

The **Carolina Parakeet** (261) is extinct. This Parakeet was North America's only native parrot. It was bright yellow-green with a yellow head and orange-red face. Its beauty made it popular as a cage bird, and its feathers were used to decorate hats. Once common in the southeastern forest, the parakeet fed on fruits and nuts. It was shot whenever it entered orchards.

Billions of **Passenger Pigeons** (262) existed during Audubon's time in the mid-1800s. The bird's head and body were bluish gray, and its breast was a warm reddish orange. Its neck was shiny greenish and red. Roosting in immense flocks in eastern forests, hundreds of Passenger Pigeons were shot by gunners who killed them for amusement. The last Passenger Pigeon died in the Cincinnati Zoo on September 1, 1914.

The **American Chestnut** (263) tree has narrowly escaped extinction. In 1906 a fungus from China entered the U.S. and killed chestnuts throughout the East. Although the fungus kills the tree above ground, the roots survive and chestnuts continue to sprout. Once a 100-foot giant of eastern forests, American Chestnut now rarely grows above 20 feet before being infected and dying back. Its leaves turn bright yellow in fall.

The **Grizzly Bear** (264) has been forced out of the lower 48 states by people. Still common in Alaska, the Grizzly is now rare over most of its former range. Its warm reddish or golden brown fur has white tipped hairs, giving it a "grizzled" appearance. The Grizzly's sloping "dished-face" separates it from the common Black Bear.

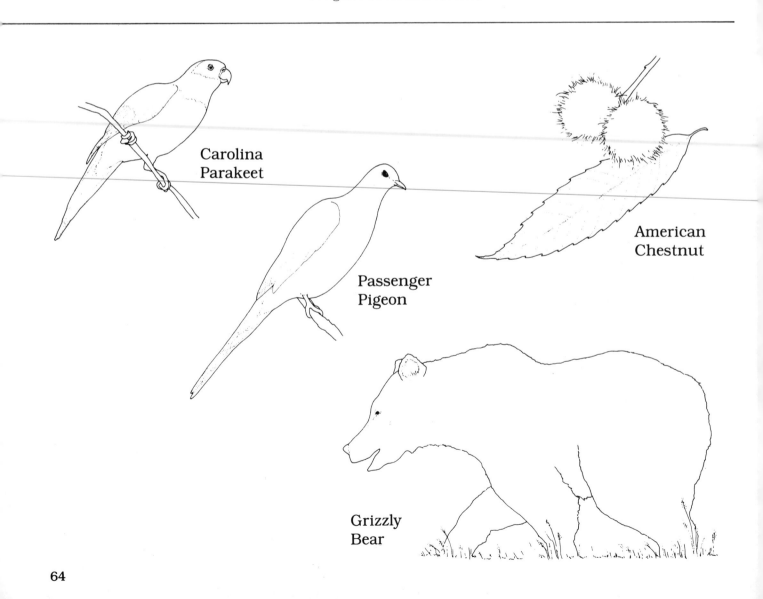

Carolina Parakeet

Passenger Pigeon

American Chestnut

Grizzly Bear

179

180

181

182

183

184

185

186

187

188

189

190

191

192

193

194

195

196

197

198

199

200

201

202

203

204

205

206

207

208

209

210

211

212

213

214

215

216

217

218

219

220

221

222

223

224

225

226

227

228

229

230

231

232

233

234

235

236